Paradiplomacy as a Diplomatic Broker

Paradiplomacy as a Diplomatic Broker

Between Separating Differences and Engaging Commonalities

By

Manuel Duran

BRILL

LEIDEN | BOSTON

Library of Congress Control Number: 2016939498

Typeface for the Latin, Greek, and Cyrillic scripts: "Brill". See and download: brill.com/brill-typeface.

ISBN 978-90-04-32592-0 (paperback)
ISBN 978-90-04-32595-1 (e-book)

Originally published as Volume 1(3) 2016, in *Diplomacy and Foreign Policy*, DOI 10.1163/24056006-12340003.

This book is printed on acid-free paper and produced in a sustainable manner.

Contents

About the Author

Manuel Duran is a Belgian political scientist and historian. He earned a master's degree in medieval history at the University of Ghent and a master's degree in International Relations & Diplomacy at the University of Antwerp. As a researcher for the Flemish Policy Research Centre on Foreign Affairs, he became interested in the diplomatic activities of sub-state political entities. His Ph.D. thesis on the subject (University of Antwerp, 2014) was published by Brill/Martinus Nijhoff as "Mediterranean Paradiplomacies. The Dynamics of Diplomatic Reterritorialization".

He is currently working as a scientific attaché at the Royal Museum of the Armed Forces and of Military History in Brussels. He has published articles on diplomacy and military history, including "An Archaeology of Mediterranean Diplomacy: the Evidence of Paradiplomacy" (*International Journal of Euro-Mediterranean Studies*, 2013).

His current research project focuses on various aspects of diplomacy in war-time periods throughout history, as well as a phenomenology of military machines as "desiring machines".

Paradiplomacy as a Diplomatic Broker

Between Separating Differences and Engaging Commonalities

Manuel Duran
University of Antwerp and Royal Army Museum, Brussels

Abstract

Since the publication of Der Derian's seminal work "On Diplomacy", diplomacy has been thought of as the mediation of estrangement between separated individuals, groups or political entities. This article focuses on paradiplomacy, the diplomatic practices of sub-state entities, as a specific site of diplomatic mediation, striking a middle ground between "realist" power play and the humanist need to connect to and engage with others. Indeed, the mediating of estrangement can be situated between both extremes of a continuum, with on the one hand absolute humanist diplomacy, aimed at rescinding all forms of separation between peoples, and on the other hand absolute power play diplomacy, maximizing these differences.

Keywords

diplomacy – paradiplomacy – antagonism – sub-state entities – homo-diplomacy

Introduction

This article deals with paradiplomacy, which can be defined as the diplomatic practices, the international activities or the foreign policy[1] of sub-state political entities, or as the "political entity's extra-jurisdictional activity targeting foreign political entities (Grydehœj 2015, 12)." Paradiplomacy first surfaced on

1 The literature on paradiplomacy often omits to differentiate between Foreign Policy as politics and Diplomacy as its procedural execution. Summarily, we might distinguish foreign relations and diplomacy as the message and the medium of international relations respectively, in which diplomacy is primarily the framework in which international relations take place, whereas foreign policy deals with the content as well as the aims and objectives of a state or other actor's relations with other states or international actors (Melissen 1999: xvii).

 | DOI 10.1163/9789004325951

the academic horizon in the late 1980s and the early 1990s, mainly as a result of the concurrent rise in European regional politics and policies, the surge of New Federalism in the Unites States and the growing Quebec and Catalan neo-nationalism. As an empirical given, it can be traced back to the 19th century (Lachapelle and Paquin 2003, 6) or even to antiquity (Duran 2013, 147–158). From the outset, paradiplomacy proved to be problematic, both in theory and in practice. First of all, it challenged the still dominant concepts of diplomacy, foreign policy and international relations as states-only phenomena. Second, and even more so, paradiplomacy has almost exclusively been studied through a number of unifocal lenses, presenting it either as an utterance of nationalistic antagonism, or as a seemingly innocent byproduct of functionalist multi-level governance or federalism. This either/or approach has proven to be very useful to expand our knowledge on the subject by adding numerous articles and books to the expanding corpus of studies on paradiplomacy, each of them highlighting one particular aspect of the diplomatic activities of substate entities. On the other hand, however, this approach has hindered seeing paradiplomacy as a mature international political practice, encompassing all aspects of a true diplomatic culture, including the search for agreement or consensus, but also the sometimes aggressive quest for self-interest at the detriment of others. This article seeks to unravel and explain the practice of paradiplomacy as the international utterance of a mature political entity. There is indeed substantial evidence that paradiplomacy has become an increasingly grown-up, global and integrated practice, one that has in other words come of age. One of the more salient aspects of this growing up process is the combination of a more realist power play and what one might label a humanist desire to connect with other peoples and political entities. As was convincingly shown by Belgian scholar David Criekemans, paradiplomacy has gone through a series of development phases, comparable to those of an infant into an adult (Criekemans, Duran and Melissen 2009). Getting into adulthood implies an increasing differentiating between Self and Other, as well as an ability to deal with the complexities of our current world. Mature paradiplomacy so becomes a specific site of diplomatic mediation, striking a middle ground between "realist" power play and the humanist need to connect to and engage with others. Indeed, the mediating of separation or estrangement can be situated between both extremes of a continuum, with on the one hand absolute humanist diplomacy (Constantinou 2009, 351–364), aimed at rescinding all forms of separation/alienation between people and peoples, and on the other hand absolute power play diplomacy, maximizing and taking advantage of these differences.

Taking the concrete diplomatic practice of a number of sub-state diplomatic actors *vis-à-vis* their international interlocutors as its point of departure, a model of description and analysis will be developed in this article to conceptualize the "separation-continuum" as an instance of the coming of age, the maturing of paradiplomacy, and the specific role of sub-state diplomatic actors therein. By focusing particularly on the integrative character of this continuum, taking into account various actors and modes of diplomacy, this article aims at strengthening our knowledge of paradiplomacy, not so much as a separate or even isolated reality of international relations, but rather as a pivot of or a broker between different actors of diplomacy, as well as between various modes of diplomatic dealing with separation and alienation. The aim is not so much to present paradiplomacy as a diplomatic "broker" between for instance the state and the sub-state political entity, but rather to consider paradiplomacy as a complex political reality, taking a middle position between attempts to break away from the state (or sometimes even the state system), and attempts to engage in the search for communalities, economic and cultural ties with other international actors, including the state. By doing so, this article is primarily aimed at diplomatic scholars and political theorists, but also at practitioners of diplomacy, being the primary actors and most prominent witnesses of the ongoing change of diplomacy as a plural, integrative and broadened international practice.

Sketching the Puzzle

On a Friday in May 2015, a small group of scholars and practitioners gathered in Brussels to discuss the present and possible future(s) of paradiplomacy.[2] During the sometimes-hefty discussions, the question was raised whether paradiplomacy had not had its best time. Not only did it look as if paradiplomacy had lost its political momentum after the "failed" Scottish and Catalan independence referenda. Also, after the prolific heydays of the 1990s and early 2000s, both the diplomatic practice and the literature on paradiplomacy now seemed to suffer from a clear fatigue. Moreover, publications on the subject proved that paradiplomacy still remained a largely neglected research object in the broader fields of IR or Foreign Policy Analysis (Bjola 2013, 7).

2 Workshop on the occasion of the book publication of "Mediterranean Paradiplomacies: Dynamics of Diplomatic Reterritorialization", May 29, 2015 in Brussels.

However true on the surface, this assessment might easily lead to epistemological reductionism, obscuring or downright denying the complexity and stratification of paradiplomacy, as a concrete emanation of political and diplomatic actorness, as well as a conceptual and theoretical given. First, paradiplomacy is not to be restricted to the diplomatic activities of a small number of regional authorities that are characterized by the presence of strong nationalist movements or political parties, as is the case in Flanders, Quebec, Scotland, Catalonia or the Basque Country. Secondly, the withering away of academic attention does by no means come down to the disappearance of a fact or event. Thirdly, remaining at the periphery of a field of study does not signify a peripheral meaning in the "real world (Gray 2009, 3–5)".

There are a number of reasons why the study (and indeed the practice) of paradiplomacy is problematic. First, a number of leading authors, such as G.R. Berridge, Maurice Keens-Soper and Thomas Otte still regard diplomacy as an exclusive prerogative of the state.[3] Second, paradiplomacy has mainly been studied from a limited number of quite idiosyncratic vantage points, primarily as an aspect of multi-level governance, of federalist or devolved state structures, or as a side effect of nationalism and/or regionalism (see below). What has been missing until now, was a theoretical framework, a template for the analysis of the sum total of the concrete international and transnational practices that one might summarize as paradiplomacy. Moreover, paradiplomacy as a research object seems to be disconnected from the findings of the broader field of Diplomatic Studies, which in itself tends to be some sort of a *Fremdkörper* in the broader academic field of International Relations. However, since a number of empirical studies have come to the conclusion that the boundaries between the practice of state and that of sub-state diplomacy are watering down (Criekemans and Duran 2010), this might open up new opportunities to integrate the conceptualizations of diplomacy and paradiplomacy. Recently, both Alexander Kuznetsov and Manuel Duran have tried to develop such an integral and integrated theory of paradiplomacy, respectively in the context of a broader study on the theory and practice of paradiplomacy (Kuznetsov 2015) and of the paradiplomatic activities of sub-state entities as an utterance of political and diplomatic reterritorialization (Duran 2015). This conjuncture of both the appearance of theoretical grounding of paradiplomacy, as well as its empirical convergence with state diplomacy, allow for more substantial thinking on paradiplomacy.

---

3 Yet, this understanding of diplomacy as a state-only practice is increasingly being replaced by that of an extended community, including sub-state and non-state actors. Diplomatic practitioners turned academics, such as Rana (2011), Petric (2013) and Mintz & DeRouen (2010) all present this new thinking (and indeed acting) of diplomacy.

This article aims at framing paradiplomacy as an instance of diplomatic mediation of separation or estrangement. Looking at diplomacy, as the management of estrangement or the mediation of separateness, has proven most fruitful since James Der Derian first put the theory forward in 1987. Yet, as Rebecca Adler-Nissen rightfully argues, it is not enough just stating diplomacy is the mediation of estrangement: "to say that diplomacy is concerned with the mediation of estrangement is only to tell part of the story" (Adler-Nissen 2015, 27). Der Derian c.s. primarily focused on the "mediating", as well as on the "alienation", but what needs to be done is precisely to unravel the various degrees of alienation, to uncover all the intensities and scales of separation. We argue that paradiplomacy, by virtue of its political and governmental weight, as well as of its place in the complex multi-level diplomatic setting that characterizes our current international landscape, lends itself to an analysis of these degrees of separation.

This article focuses on paradiplomacy as a specific site of diplomatic mediation, striking a middle ground between "realist" power play and the humanist need to connect to and engage with others. Indeed, the mediating of estrangement can be situated between both extremes of a continuum, with on the one hand absolute humanist diplomacy (Constantinou 2010), aimed at rescinding all forms of separation/alienation between people and peoples, and on the other hand absolute power play diplomacy, maximizing these differences. Certain instances of traditional state diplomacy—by virtue of its historical development as an instrument of state formation—can be situated on the power play diplomatic side of the continuum, while the diplomatic activities of churches, individuals, NGO's and cities are to be found on the humanist diplomatic side of the continuum. The primary goal of the first is to defend and promote the interests of the state *vis-à-vis* other international actors, while the primary goal of the latter tends to be the creation of various forms of connectivity with other people and peoples. We might therefore label power play diplomacy as site of political heterology, i.e. a dynamic whereby a political actor bases his actions on, and wishes to maintain or even intensify, the various differences between people and peoples. Humanist diplomacy on the other hand can be considered a site of political homology, being the quest for diminishing separation between people and peoples by stressing the commonalities that exist between human beings and by transcending political borders.

As a result of its governmental middle ground positioning, paradiplomacy often holds an intermediate position between power play and humanist diplomacy. Sub-state entities do defend the interest(s) of (the inhabitants of) their territory and its socio-economic positioning in the contemporary globalized configuration, and as such compete with other sub-state entities and other internationally active political actors. On the other hand, they often strengthen—both in practice and in discourse—political, cultural, social and economic ties with other sub-state entities and with other internationally active actors. As a result of their specific political gravity, they also function as pivots of various instances of homologic diplomacy, functioning as a mediator between different peoples.

In the following paragraphs, this article will try to solve the above mentioned puzzle. First, this article offers a concise overview of the literature on paradiplomacy, highlighting the various and diverse, but often one-dimensional approaches towards the subject. It then paints a canvas of what I would like to call "Der Derian's turn", the new take on diplomacy since the publication of James Der Derian's influential work and how this turn can also be made in the study of paradiplomacy. Paradiplomacy can be looked at as a specific dynamics of separation, consisting of protagonists and antagonists, as well as the particular—or even peculiar—rules and customs. Third, we take a look at a number of concrete sites of paradiplomatic practice in order to validate our claim that paradiplomacy can be better (or even best) be understood as a particular site within the separation continuum.

Conceptualizing Paradiplomacy

The emergence of sub-state entities since the 1970s is an expression of a new form of political actorness within the framework of the global diplomatic landscape, in which numerous types of sub-state entities such as municipalities, provinces, counties and regions have increasingly gained attributes that were hitherto reserved for the state, as they carved out new and often quite considerable prerogatives, powers and even legal-constitutional competences (Brubaker 2004, 157). One of these attributes has been the right to develop one's own international policies and diplomacies. Indeed, since the early 1980s, an increasing number of sub-state entities developed their own diplomatic and foreign policy apparatus, parallel to or sometimes even competing with that of the central state. It needs to be acknowledged here however that sub-states are but one of the many non-state actors that have surfaced in the diplomatic realm during the last decades. Cities (Acuto 2013), rogue states, NGO's (Betsill and Corell 2008), multinational corporations, as well as influential individuals all make up the increasingly plural international landscape. What separates sub-state entities, as well as cities, from other non-state diplomatic actors is their territorial character, in that they represent, communicate and act on behalf of the inhabitants of a specific territorial configuration, be it a region, a province or an autonomous community.

The last decades, the political actorness of sub-state entities, as well as their diplomatic activities have drawn considerable attention, from scholars and practitioners alike. One could say, there has been a real proliferation of academic and policy-relevant literature on the topic of paradiplomacy. The founding fathers of theory building on the subject were Panayotis Soldatos, who coined and defined the term 'paradiplomacy' as the diplomatic practices of sub-state entities,[4] and Ivo Duchacek, who initially talked about micro-diplomacy (Duchacek 1990). The first has developed an analytical system distinguishing between domestic determinants on the regional level (objective segmentation, perceptual segmentation (electoralism), regionalism/nationalism, asymmetry of federated units, growth of federated units, 'me-tooism'), domestic determinants on the federal level (federal errors / inefficiency, problems with the nation-building process, institutional gap, constitutional uncertainties, foreign policy domestication) and external causes (global interdependence, involvement of external actors, regional interdependence) (Soldatos 1990, 45). The latter distinguished three categories of diplomatic practice: (1) cross-border regional paradiplomacy, such as institutionalized in the European regions through the Euroregions; (2) trans-regional paradiplomacy, or institutionalized contacts between sub-national authorities that have no geographical boundaries (a notable example are the so-called Four Motors for Europe, four highly industrialized regions that pool their diplomatic apparatus and work closely together in a great number of cooperation projects and programs: Catalonia, Baden-Württemberg, Rhône-Alpes, and Lombardy); and (3) global diplomacy, or direct contacts between sub-state authorities of different countries, or between a central and a sub-state authority, or between a sub-state authority and a private actor. Building further on Duchacek and Soldatos, Eric Philippart developed a new typology of paradiplomacy, consisting of five categories of diplomacy: minimal, minor, major, and maximal paradiplomacy, as well as the even more problematic category of proto-diplomacy. Minimal paradiplomacy is limited to cross-border cooperation, focusing on socio-economic and cultural cooperation. Minor paradiplomacy is based on cross-border cooperation, including the opening of economic representations. Major paradiplomacy has an unlimited geographical scope; it also includes political cooperation. The French region of Rhône-Alpes practices this kind of paradiplomacy (including through the Four Motors for Europe), as do most Spanish and Italian regions. Maximal paradiplomacy is often generated by

4 The word "paradiplomacy" was first used by diplomatic historian Rohan Butler in 1961, who defined it as the exercise of "personal and parallel diplomacy complementing or competing with the regular foreign policy of the government". See Butler 1961, 12.

strong regionalism and nationalism, and is aimed at strengthening the regional benefits. The Basque Country, as well as Catalonia and Quebec are good examples of sub-state entities practicing this kind of paradiplomacy. Finally, the problematic concept of 'proto-diplomacy' is the transit phase towards independence. Philippart mentions here, with some sense of exaggeration, the Belgian regions (Phillipart 1998).

An important contribution to the theory of paradiplomacy was developed by Stéphane Paquin. He bases himself on the maximalist concept of Philippart, but instead calls it 'identitary paradiplomacy'. The main difference between identitary paradiplomacy and proto-diplomacy is that the first does not have the final objective of independence, unlike proto-diplomacy. According to Paquin, nationalism is the main independent variable in the study of paradiplomacy. It is, however, not the sole or even primary variable, which are often processes of economic development (as with the German *Länder* or most U.S. states). Since nationalism is not the only relevant variable, Paquin attempts to determine under what conditions paradiplomacy is conflictual or rather cooperative? He identifies a number of indicators that demonstrate the variable 'conflict': disputes before the national constitutional courts; divergent international positions; 'diplomatic opposition'; perceptions; and discourse. Indicators that demonstrate collaboration are: bilateral agreements between central and sub-state governments on international relations; organization of joint events; and finally perception (Paquin 2004).

In his article 'Paradiplomacy: Reflections on the Foreign Policy and International Relations of Regions', André Lecours identifies the causes of paradiplomacy on both the domestic political level and at the international level (Lecours 2002). His analytical framework of paradiplomacy reflects domestic and international determinants in a multi-layered domestic and foreign context, consisting of regional political systems, national structures, continental regimes, and the overall global system, each of which are opportunity structures for the international activities of sub-national authorities. By doing so, Lecours was the first to offer an integrative and comprehensive analytical and theoretical framework to explain the causalities and the opportunity structures that account for the advent of paradiplomacy.

While these theoretical perspectives are primarily of an explanatory nature, mainly searching for causality between domestic as well as external factors and sub-state diplomatic practices, a number of recent publications have brought the concrete practice of diplomacy back to the study of paradiplomacy. They focus on paradiplomacy as a means to deal with and overcome the limitations set by boundaries between social groupings, be they of a geographical nature (such as rivers, mountain passes and seas), of a juridical nature (state borders and borders between infra-state territorial entities), or of a cultural and even psychological nature. Brian Hocking was the first to offer a new approach to the study of paradiplomacy, by presenting the concept of multilayered or catalytic diplomacy (Hocking 1993 and Hocking 1999). This concept presents sub-state political authorities as full-fledged international actors. Catalytic diplomacy, according to Hocking, is to be considered as a web of ever shifting interactions between different players, depending on the policy domain, interests and the capacity to operate in such an environment. In doing so, sub-state entities are not only changing the rules of diplomacy by allowing more than only states to play, but also the nature of the game by altering relations among the different players, leaving more room for flexible, fluent and improvised patterns of diplomacy. In this catalytic diplomacy, sub-state entities become bridge-builders and gatekeepers within an increasingly complex diplomatic matrix that spans all sorts of actors across the globe (Hocking 1995).

As already mentioned, David Criekemans has developed an analytical matrix to analyze and evaluate the myriad of diplomatic instruments and variations in the organizational structure of diplomacy and foreign policy within different sub-state entities (Criekemans 2010a). This has not only advanced our knowledge of the concrete elaboration and development of paradiplomacy, but has also given rise to a more historical conceptualization of paradiplomacy as an evolving practiced concept of political reality, subject to constant and contingent change. Criekemans distinguishes three phases or waves in the development of sub-state diplomacy.

> The first wave manifested itself from the 1980s onwards: a growing number of non-central governments tried to attract foreign direct investment through own initiatives [...] or to use culture and identity as a lever to place oneself on the international map. The second wave in the 1990s was characterized by the creation, within the sub-state entities of certain (European) countries, of a judicially grounded set of instruments for their own (parallel as well as complementary) diplomatic activities [...]. The current third wave is characterized by steps towards a 'verticalization' of the organizational structure of the administration or department of external/foreign affairs, a strategic reorientation of the geopolitical and functional priorities, and attempts to integrate the external instruments of a sub-state foreign policy into a well-performing whole (Criekemans, Duran and Melissen 2009, 6).

This presentation of paradiplomacy is particularly important since it allows for a historical view on paradiplomacy as an evolving, maturing diplomatic and political given. Parag Khanna sees growing importance for the role of non-state actors, including sub-state entities, in the new diplomatic environment of the twenty-first century, which he calls 'mega-diplomacy', in that it includes not only states, cities, firms, religions, individuals, regions, NGOs, universities but all institutions that feel called upon. Mega-diplomacy is not so much about affirming the separateness of each nation through traditional diplomacy and sovereign representation, but about creating unity across communities to manage our collective space (Khanna 2011, 22). Mega-diplomacy is characterized by three principles: (1) inclusiveness: getting all hands on deck, through the multi-stakeholder involvement of governments, companies and NGOs, (2) decentralization: spreading capabilities widely, and as close to problems as possible, thus promoting empowerment and resilience; (3) mutual accountability: building communities of trust among participants, creating obligations to one another and the mission (Khanna 2011, 23).

Noé Cornago has through the years been dealing with the theory and practice of paradiplomacy. He analyzed the global character of all the instances of sub-state diplomacy, encompassing the diplomacies of sub-state entities on all continents, mainly in Europe and Northern America, where it originated, but also increasingly in Latin America, Asia and Africa (Cornago 2000c). This global diffusion of paradiplomatic practices has also engendered more acceptance of paradiplomacy, notably with regard to the adaptation of practices, institutions and discourses:

> It is noteworthy, for instance, how easily adaptable the practices, institutions and discourses of sub-state diplomacy have proven, even in the most disparate contexts. This ease reveals an interesting process of policy learning and reflective adaptation to the changing structural contexts alongside sub-state governments worldwide (Cornago 2010a, 27).
>
> The globalization of sub-state diplomacy, as well as the easy adaptation of sub-state diplomatic practices, have made it a transformative power in world politics, in that it presents and represents the hitherto silenced diversity of voices and practices that constitute a wider understanding of diplomacy as the experience of encountering and dealing with 'otherness' (Cornago 2010b, 89).

A already mentioned, recent contributions to the study of paradiplomacy have been made by Alexander Kuznetsov and Manuel Duran. Their research aims at providing an integrated perspective describing and explaining the main characteristics of paradiplomacy, as well as to tackle the questions of why, how and to what effect paradiplomacy is practiced. Kuznetsov constructs, through a systematisation of the different approaches in understanding the practice of paradiplomacy, an integrative theoretical explanatory framework to guide research on regional governments' involvement in international affairs. Duran presents a new view on paradiplomacy by analyzing the diplomatic activities of a number of Mediterranean sub-state entities as a site of political territorialization. In his book, he shows that the international actorness of these sub-state entities is giving way to new patterns of territorialization, as well as alternative forms of diplomacy. Both authors signal the need for paradiplomacy specialists to engage more with the broader Diplomatic Studies community:

> Thus, it seems there is a strong incentive to do research on regional governments' involvement in international affairs, because there are various white spots on the map of paradiplomacy studies that have not been discovered or tackled until today (Kuznetsov 2015, 4).

In other words, the study of paradiplomacy does seem to be in need of a new impulse, focusing more on the relationship between paradiplomatic activities and the broader practice and study field of diplomacy. The nexus of this new impulse might well be found in what can be considered the most important turning point in the study of diplomacy in the last half-century, the alienation turn of James Der Derian.

Der Derian's Turn—Mediating Alienation

In the 1980s, coincidentally at the height of the growing academic interest for paradiplomacy, American scholar James Der Derian made way with traditional thinking about diplomacy. Thinking and writing about diplomacy had for a long time been the prerogative of professional diplomats, legal scholars and historians. Authors such as Ernest Mason Satow, Eileen Denza, and Harold Nicolson dominated the literature on the subject with titles ranging from *A Guide to Diplomatic Practice* (Satow 1932), and *Diplomatic Law* (Denza 2004) to *The Evolution of Diplomacy* (Nicolson 1962). Notwithstanding the undeniable value[5] and scholarly qualities of these texts, they all suffered from a lack of theory building and analytical conceptualization. This was mainly due to the fact that, in an academic context, diplomacy was often imbedded in the historical and legal departments, as well as to the inclination of the diplomatic

5 As well as literary merits, a quality that is—alas—increasingly ignored and sidelined as being irrelevant.

practitioners to the day-to-day activities that determined their vision on all things diplomatic. The main aim of these authors was not so much to look for the ontological meaning of diplomacy, but rather to either present a hands-on manual for future diplomats or rendering a narrative of the historical coming into being of modern diplomacy from the Peace of Westphalia up to the present times (Black 2010, 10–12).

All of this changed, rather dramatically one might say, with the publication in 1987 of a remarkable book by American political scientist James Der Derian. In this book, entitled *On Diplomacy*, he presented what he called a genealogy of diplomacy as a means to build a solid theoretical base of the phenomenon. Der Derian's book proved to be a watershed in the conceptualization of diplomacy as an international practice.

The genealogical method was developed by Michel Foucault as a method of social and historic enquiry to unravel all sorts of social and political phenomena.[6] Foucault's genealogical method was highly influenced by Friedrich Nietzsche's genealogy as a means to disentangle moral and ethical systems through the lens of power relations and power structures (Nietzsche 2013). It would lead us too far, and it is not the aim of this article, to divulge all the details of the genealogic method, let alone the subtleties of Foucaultian thinking. Yet it is important to get at least a basic understanding of what this method entails. It basically is a way at looking at contemporary social (or political) phenomena by focusing on the one hand on both the language (the discourse) that is used to talk about these phenomena and the structures of knowledge that are presented through these discourses, and on the other hand on the power structures that are revealed through, but also constructed through language and knowledge. Power structures, in other words, are made up of discursive practices that ground these structures. To truly understand a social practice, we must therefore look at the ways in which these social practices are talked about, past and present, and what power structures lie underneath this coding, encoding and recoding. Discourse and power are linked as follows:

> In truth these two tasks are never completely separable…The regular formation of discourse can incorporate the procedures of control, in certain conditions and to a certain extent (that is what happens, for

6 The topics that Foucault subjected to his genealogical method were as diverse as the emergence of the modern prison system (*Surveiller et punir: naissance de la prison*), the evolution of sexual practices (*Histoire de la sexualité*) or the human body as a political phenomenon (*Naissance de la biopolitique*).

> instance, when a discipline takes on the form and status of a scientific discourse); and conversely the figures of control can take shape within a discursive formation ... The difference between the critical and the genealogical enterprise is not so much a difference of object or domain, but of point of attack, perspective and delimitation (Foucault 1981, 70).

That is exactly what James Der Derian set out to do, looking at what lies beneath and behind past and present discourses on diplomacy. Unlike his predecessors, who focused on the historical and legal development of diplomatic practices and principles, such as the coming into being of the resident ambassador, and diplomatic reciprocity or the principles of extraterritoriality and immunity, Der Derian looked for the answer to the "why-" question: why did and do people engage in "the second oldest profession in the world"? The answer he came up with was provocative in its simplicity, yet at the same time daring in its complexity. People and groupings of people do diplomacy in order to mediate the various degrees of estrangement or alienation that exist between them. As individuals and as being part of one group or another, humans experience different forms of alienation or estrangement: they talk another language, practice a different religion; they are rich or poor, old or young; but they also inhabit a different part of this earth and organize themselves in different families, boroughs, cities, regions and nations. Whenever an individual or a group of people encounters another individual or another group of people, they have to deal with, to manage the differences that exist between them. They, in other words, have to come to grips with the various degrees of estrangement, of alienation that exist between them. This management of estrangement is a delicate balancing act. When it becomes too outspoken, too radical, estrangement might result in a total shutdown or meltdown of the relations and even communication lines between individuals and groups. This in turn greatly increases the hazard of miscommunication and misinterpretations of each other's deeds and words and lowers the threshold for tensions and conflicts, yes, even war. On the other hand, when the estrangement between individuals and groups of people were to be too limited, too small, this would mean the end of an individual's or group's singularity. When there is no alienation, no estrangement whatsoever between humans, they cease to be truly individual. Estrangement, alienation is as such an integral part of the *condition humaine*: it has to be there to a certain extent, but it has to be managed properly in order for it not to become too risky. And this is where diplomacy comes in. The instrument *par excellence* to deal with these degrees of estrangement, the tool to do this balancing act between too outspoken and too limited, is diplomacy. After all, from the outset, and in spite of substantial geographic and historical differences, the essence of diplomacy was, is and should be the acknowledgement of the other's differences and the subsequent search for commonalities, in compromising antagonistic interests and harmonizing conflicting principles. Without this basic mentality, diplomacy will inevitably lead to either a naive desire to wipe out all differences between people and peoples, or an aggressive inclination to enlarge and reinforce these differences and thus disabling any form of commonality.

Der Derian's theory was further developed by Paul Sharp in his "Diplomatic Theory of International Relations", in which he rephrases the alienation-theory of Der Derian as relations of separateness that exist between people and peoples, regardless of their character:

> We may be uncertain as to when relations of separateness are likely to occur, and we may be clearer that they are produced and that they do not simply naturally occur, yet at any given moment, they are occurring and they are being produced. As to whether they are a good thing or not, for diplomats, this question is almost as meaningless as asking the same about the weather (Sharp 2009, 88).

Hussein Banai (2014) signals the lack of engagement with historical narratives and memories that underlie the various relations in world politics. Diplomacy here becomes an instance of mediating not so much the various degrees of separation between people and groups of people, but of mediating the public imagination(s) in world society.

With their innovative and unconventional approach, both James Der Derian, Paul Sharp, Hussein Banai and others with them, have revitalized the study of diplomacy substantively. Their work liberated diplomacy from the strict confinements of formal and formalist inter-state relations. The study of diplomacy increasingly connected with the growing complexity and multiplicity of diplomacy's practice in a fast changing world. This new diplomatic practice not only included non-state diplomatic actors and non-formal diplomatic activities, but also a new and broadened diplomatic agenda (Riordan 2002). Strangely enough, however, neither Der Derian nor Sharp or Banai pay much attention to paradiplomacy, a very outspoken instance of this new diplomatic practice. Could this be because both of them still adhere to the (neo-) classical taking on international relations as being fundamentally separated from domestic politics, thereby ignoring the interplay between domestic complexity and diplomacy (Cornago 2013, 1)?

The Turn in Paradiplomacy: A Dynamics of Separation

We argue that paradiplomacy might indeed benefit from a conceptual turn, comparable to the one the publication of "On Diplomacy" brought about in the realm of Diplomatic Studies. When turned this way, paradiplomacy might become one of the paradigmatic sites of diplomacy-as-management-of-alienation or separation, precisely because it can be found, both in practice and discourse, on the sometimes-narrow intersection between international and domestic, between inside and outside. This separation dynamic has three key aspects: first, the protagonists, being sub-state entities engaging in diplomatic relations; second, the antagonists, being the others (with or without capital O) or diplomatic interlocutors of sub-state entities; and third, the separation dynamic itself with its specific course, rules, customs and pace.

First, we have to consider the protagonists of the separation dynamics, the political sub-state actors that practice paradiplomacy. Sub-state political entities can be defined as 'a coherent territorial entity situated between local and national levels with a capacity for authoritative decision-making' (Marks, Hooghe and Schakel 2008, 113). This includes entities such as provinces (Canada), cantons (Switzerland), *Länder* (Germany and Austria), states (the United States, Australia and Brazil), Autonomous Communities (Spain) or regions (Chile, Belgium, France and Italy). The emergence of sub-state entities has become increasingly common, reflecting the growing twentieth-century reality of limitations of state sovereignty and political territoriality (Elazar 1987, 225). Sub-state entities can have a strong historical pedigree, like the Spanish "historical nationalities" Catalonia, the Basque Country and Galicia, the French region of Brittany, the Belgian region of Flanders, the Italian region of Tuscany, the German Land of Bavaria or Scotland. Others can be primarily administrative sub-units of a state, such as the Hungarian planning and statistical regions, the Portuguese districts, or the regions of Chile. Some sub-state entities consist of the merging of two or more sub-state entities, such as the French regions of Languedoc-Roussillon-Midi-Pyrénées and Auvergne-Rhone-Alpes,[7]

7 French regions were originally designed as administrative units for spatial planning. For this purpose, 22 planning regions were set up in 1956. They more or less resembled the pre-revolutionary provinces. Unlike departments and the communes, regions were not designed as territorial collectivities. This only happened following the adoption of the decentralization law of 16 March 1986. As of January 2016, French regions are reduced to 18 by merging certain existing regions. Nord-Pas de Calais and Picardy for instance will merge into Nord-Pas de Calais-Picardy. High and Low Normandy will be merged into Normandy.

the Italian region of Emilia-Romagna, the Canadian province of Newfoundland and Labrador, or the German Land of Mecklenburg-Vorpommern. Some sub-state entities have considerable competences, domestically as well as in the international domain. Notable examples are the Belgian regions. The Flemish and Walloon regions, as well as the Brussels-Capital Region possess competences relating to the economy, employment, agriculture, water policy, housing, public works, energy, public transport, the environment, town and country planning, nature conservation, credit, foreign trade, and supervision of the lower-tier administrative units, such as the communes and the provinces. Through the "in foro interno, in foro externo"-principle (see below), they also have powers relating international relations in those fields. Others have limited, primarily administrative powers, such as the Algerian *Willayas* (provinces) or the Luxemburg districts. Some sub-state entities are incorporated in a complex system of asymmetrical decentralization, as is the case with Spanish autonomous communities. Spain is an asymmetrical federation, since each autonomous community has negotiated (or has to negotiate if it wants to revise) its statute separately with Madrid. As such, a general delimitation of the autonomous regions' competences does not exist, but according to articles 147 and 148 of the Spanish Constitution, it is possible to discern three types of competences: competences exclusively relating to the central state; mixed competences; and exclusive regional competences.

Some sub-state entities have an impressive historical "track record" when it comes to their diplomatic activities, sometimes going back as far as the Middle Ages. The Crown of Aragon, of which Catalonia was a principality, for example was responsible for the 'Consulate of the Sea', the codification of maritime and commercial law, as well as a body of judicial representations that spread throughout the entire Mediterranean basin and which were directly based upon Catalan's maritime customs. The government of the autonomous community of Catalonia has revived this Consulate of the Sea. It is now a commercial arbitration service that is operated by the Chamber of Commerce of Barcelona, as well as a network of commercial promotion offices abroad. As divers as they might be, all these sub-state entities can be regarded as the protagonists in the separation dynamics, confronting them to a myriad of antagonists, ranging from foreign interlocutors, such as foreign regions and states or multilateral forums such as the UN, to domestic partners/competitors, being the state they belong to, co-regions of that state or lower-tier political entities, such as cities and provinces.

The second element of the separation dynamics is thus this rather unequivocal multiplicity of paradiplomacy's Others/outside(s). These can be regarded as the antagonists in the separation dynamics. Paradiplomacy has a multilayered outside, that can be broken down in three layers of an expanding outside.

> Above all, in—but surely not exclusively limited to—the European Union, sub-state authorities have been adopting a three-sided strategy to enhance their international stance, aimed at the national, the EU, and the international (or transnational) level (Duran 2015, 271).

The first stratum of the outside lies within the context (or the confinements) of the states of which sub-state entities are a constitutive part. Both co-regional authorities and the central government form the first layer of the diplomatic Other of sub-state diplomacies. It is here that the territorial exclusivity of the state is being reshaped by sub-state actors that are constructing new patterns of political space (Zanon 2011, 329). The second stratum of the paradiplomatic outside consists of its dealings at the supranational or intraregional level, notably the various EU institutions, such as the Committee of the Regions, but also of sub-state entities' involvement in the many strands of EU-initiated territorial policies. These include the various cross-border, transnational and interregional programs, as well as the new territorial constructs that are the Euroregions and the macro-regions. These territorial policies, although best known in a EU context, are certainly not limited to the European political and economic space. Also the North-American space for instance is being transformed by territorial policies (Schacter, Beebe and Zanasi 2004). The third layer consists of the various ways in which all the other diplomatic interlocutors are being approached by means of network and organization diplomacy, as well as bilateral and multilateral contacts, and also in the context of decentralized development cooperation or sub-state foreign aid. This is the place where regional authorities are at their most autonomous, in that they are not embedded in the national diplomatic frameworks, which still play a strong role in the first two layers, but (try to) act in their own right and in their own name.

These three strata make up the concentric and overlapping circles of sub-state diplomatic socialization, in which sub-state entities engage with: (1) their nearby outside (the central state and co-regions); (2) the European—or other supranational—outside (the various EU and NAFTA territorial programs and groupings); and (3) the international outside (geographic and functional international networks and organizations). Moreover, paradiplomacy qua diplomacy has a distinct ambivalent character. Both "in practice and discursively paradiplomacy suggests a desire to emulate official diplomacy whilst simultaneously affirming a distinctive will of political autonomy (Cornago 2013, 3)".

The third element to be considered, next to the protagonists and the antagonists, is the separation dynamics itself. Paradiplomacy is situated between humanist and realist power play diplomatic logics. This is the core of the separation dynamics, the rules, the course, pace and customs of the dynamic. Here the various instances of separation and alienation are being played out, the protagonists and antagonists figuring as pieces in a game of chess. And just as with a game, the outcome is unsure and the process is a dynamic, shifting one. This will be further developed in the next paragraph.

The Separation Dynamics: Degrees or Instances of Separation

This paragraph mainly aims at disseminating the empirical material, offering an overview of the various degrees of separation that result from or on the contrary generate patterns of paradiplomacy. The various instances, degrees of separation make out the "separation dynamics". These degrees of separation are to be situated on a continuum, ranging from maximum heterological to extreme homological diplomacy.

Diplomatic heterology is one end of the spectrum in the separation dynamics. Heterology, according to the dictionary means "not corresponding or similar in position, value, structure, or function" or "dissimilarity, unsimilarity—the quality of being dissimilar." One of the theorists of heterology as a philosophical and sociological category was French philosopher Georges Bataille, who regarded heterology a key element of identity formation, both on an individual and a collective level, even as the difference that must be expelled from the same in order for the same to be the same (Wernick 1999). Heterology in a diplomatic context is about maximizing its own interests, or even its own international identity at the detriment of its diplomatic partners. Taken to the extreme, it results in the sort of diplomatic isolation certain international pariahs are confronted with and whose relations with the outward world were described by Paul Sharp as "rogue state diplomacy (Sharp 2009, 195)."

Homology, the opposite of heterology, on the other hand is a likeness, a similarity or a correspondence in structure. Homology as a site of diplomatic encounters and relationships has been conceptualized and theorized by Costas Costantinou, who even coined the term "homo-diplomacy" to describe the human dimension of diplomacy, that is to say, the interpersonal dealings of the homo sapiens, or the experimental and experiential diplomacy of everyday life (Constantinou 2006, 351).

Homo- or humanist diplomacy, instead of stressing the divergences, the differences and the adversities between a diplomatic Self and its diplomatic Other(s), is aimed at strengthening and advocating diplomatic—and indeed—human sameness. It is a way to defuse conflicts, an instrument of peace building and a means to bring peoples and people closer together via concrete diplomatic actions.

As will be shown below, the concrete practice of paradiplomacy is to be found on a continuum between maximum heterological and extreme homological diplomacy. This "middle ground" is not to be regarded as a static line of possible policy choices and outcomes, but rather a sliding scale shifting from coercion to engagement, from political and diplomatic hegemony to political communality and diplomatic solidarity—and back. The driving force of this extension of the epistemic community of diplomacy is the public expectation manifested by the Global Square of Globalization. Both absolute homology, or the unconditional engagement of commonalities, and absolute heterology, being the pure separating of differences are to be considered as theoretic ideal types, rather than actual policy positions. They are used here as the ends of an analytical yardstick to get a grip on what is first and foremost a dynamic of shifting concepts, policies, and even polities (in that also the territoriality of sub-state entities, and what this entails for their diplomatic practice and vision, is also subject to "variable geometries"). What paradiplomacy does is on the one hand mediate between various diplomatic actors, state, sub-state and other non-state, but rather between the two poles of diplomacy-as-a-practice, a realist pole (agonism) and a humanist pole (looking for connectivity, also with the state). The mediation is not exclusively between actors per se, but also between modes of diplomatic practice.

Heterology

Diplomatic heterology, particularly in the field of paradiplomacy, can take on different forms. This article examines three expressions of paradiplomatic heterology: antagonistic paradiplomacy, the emergence of counter-embassies, and finally—and related to both antagonistic and counter-diplomacy—the phenomenon of diplomatic mimicry. All three have in common that they are being used and played out in order to position and emphasize the diplomatic identity and position of the protagonist in question at the detriment of the diplomatic other(s), particularly the central state these sub-state entities belong to. In doing so, they make out one half of the separation dynamic. Political antagonism relates to the way in which sub-state entities make use of their diplomatic apparatus to set themselves apart from and even oppose the central state they are part of. This particular site of paradiplomacy is primarily fuelled by nationalist political parties of movements, for instance in Catalonia, the Basque Country and Scotland. One specific means of diplomatic differentiation in the setting up of a network of counter-, or pseudo-embassies in order to compete with the official embassies. A telling example are the counter-embassies that originated from the Russian Revolution of 1917. Setting up competing embassies is a clear example of the dynamic of diplomatic mimicry, the sum of institutions and practices aimed at emulating state diplomacy, with a particular emphasis on diplomatic protocol, diplomatic bureaucracy and presidential visits.

1 *Political Antagonism—Nationalism*

Paradiplomacy is often studied through the lens of nationalist antagonism, whereby the diplomatic practices as they are performed by sub-state entities with strong nationalist movements, are a concrete instrument in the political competition with the central state these sub-state entities belong to. Paradigmatic (and often cited) examples are Catalonia, Scotland, Flanders, the Basque Country and Quebec, all of them considered as "stateless nations". 'Stateless nation' is, besides a conceptual given, a highly political term, asserting the legitimate claims for secession or extensive autonomy for a group that considers itself to be a nation entitled to its own state.[8] In recent history, the development of paradiplomacy has been influenced by or has been an instrument in the organisation of referenda on more sovereignty or downright independence in a least three cases namely the Canadian province of Quebec, the Spanish autonomous community of Catalonia and the British devolved nation of Scotland. These referenda have become instances of heightened political and diplomatic heterology, in which state and sub-state have found themselves at opposites sites of an invisible barrier: both sides at a certain point were more engaged in convincing the international and diplomatic community of their own right than in communicating and negotiating with the other side. We will therefore take a look at exactly these three cases, Quebec, Catalonia and Scotland to analyse this highly heterological take on paradiplomacy.

The first stateless nation to actively make use of its diplomatic activities and foreign policy apparatus to further its state-building goals, more often than not to the detriment of or in a tensed relationship with the central state, was the Canadian province of Quebec. The sum total of their external relations can even be considered an important precedent (Rutan 1971) or even the 'graduate school of paradiplomacy (Duchacek 1986, 248)'. The genesis of Quebec's paradiplomacy is to be found in the fundamental societal shift that was the so-called Quiet Revolution of the 1960s, which was characterized by the retreat of the Catholic Church as the political centre of gravity, the coming into

8 See *inter alia* Keating 2001, Paquin 2003, Grydehoj 2014 and Kuznetsov 2015.

being of the welfare state and the surge of Quebec regionalism and nationalism.[9] Especially during and after the liberal Lesage government of 1960–1966 and the proclamation of the Gérin-Lajoie doctrine, that stated that what is Quebec's jurisdiction at home is Quebec's jurisdiction abroad, Quebec's paradiplomacy gained a momentum it would never really lose. Over the years Quebec has developed an impressive paradiplomatic apparatus, consisting of a ministry of international relations, a considerable bilateral and multilateral representational network,[10] as well as a concrete diplomatic policy, based on a great number of international projects, and programs.[11] Moreover, Quebec is actively pushing the limits of paradiplomacy by appropriating certain aspects of what is traditionally considered the prerogatives of states in the global international arena, especially in the fields of security, notably border control policies and the economy-energy nexus.

Quebec also practices a form of diplomacy that is greatly based on state diplomacy, with a great emphasis on international agreements and international law,[12] diplomatic protocol, the scrupulous application of diplomatic norms and customs, a formalized form of diplomatic communication. This diplomatic communication took a distinct heterological turn during the referenda of 1980 and 1995, opposing those in favour of Quebec independence and those advocating Canadian unity. Paradiplomacy became instrumental, especially during the running-up to the 1995 referendum, for the state-to-be of the Quebec nation, defined by Bernard Landry, then Quebec minister of international affairs as "the place where democracy is practiced, where social relations and arbitration are played and where the citizen has the greatest opportunity to take part in the decisions that affect him or her (Bélanger 1997, 49–50)." The aftermath of both referenda proved to be a difficult adjustment process, with painful pronouncements, especially by Jacques Parizeau, Premier of Quebec and Leader of the "Yes" Committee, who stated that the "No"-camp had prevailed only thanks to "money and ethnic votes (Cardinal 2005, 398)."

---

9 The genesis of Quebec's paradiplomacy has an even older pedigree, dating back to the nineteenth century, when the province set its first steps on the international arena, see: Stéphane Paquin and Guy Lachapelle 2005, 77.

10 This diplomatic network is characterized by an organizational modulation with 7 general delegations (government offices), 4 delegations (government offices), 8 bureaus, 3 trade offices and 2 areas of representation in multilateral affairs (within UNESCO and the International Organisation of the Francophonie.

11 For a concise overview of Quebec's diplomatic apparatus, see: Manuel Duran, David Criekemans and Jan Melissen 2009, 15–70.

12 Up to this day, more than 700 international agreements have been signed by the Quebec government.

This same combination of highly formalized and (even more outspoken) antagonistic paradiplomacy is to be found in the Spanish autonomous community of Catalonia. This political antagonism has undergone a clear radicalisation since the genesis of Catalonia's diplomacy during the 1980s. Jordi Pujol, the longstanding president of the Catalan *Generalitat* (the combination of both the Catalan executive, the president and the parliament), is considered the 'godfather' of Catalan sub-state diplomacy and foreign policies. Indeed, his presidency was one that particularly aimed at enhancing Catalonia's stature in the overall Spanish political space as well as in the global realm. From the outset, Pujol recognized the importance of a foreign audience and external partners to achieve his domestic goals. He was not only the prime architect of Catalonia's diplomatic practices—including the establishment of diplomatic offices abroad, the signing of international treaties, and embedding Catalonia in as many international organizations and networks as possible—but was also one of the key political thinkers and even ideologues on Catalonia's place on the international map. Over the years, during his presidency (that lasted from 1980 until 2003) as well as afterwards, Pujol turned out to be a prolific writer on diverse topics such as Catalan identity and history, Europe, the economic crisis, religion, spirituality and the importance of education. His latest publication, shortly before the outbreak of the corruption scandal in which he and his family was involved, is a comparative study of the place of Catalonia in Spain, in which he states the case for more autonomy within a Spanish context, as is the case in Canada for Quebec:

> At any rate, between independence and being the Spanish Quebec, many people would vote for the latter. But it may well be that for Spain the status of Quebec is as unacceptable as independence. While we await the day of a hypothetical officially binding referendum, the Catalans do have one clear objective: to strengthen ourselves internally. We need to strengthen our economy, our cultural creativity, our civil society. Without expecting any help or justice. Yet with the confidence we have in one fact: in Catalonia we have a country. There are people with initiatives. Now as well, despite the crisis and Spanish hostility. And if we have a country we have a future. And day by day the country will use its right to decide (Pujol 2011).

More radical in his stance towards both Catalan independence and the role of diplomacy in gaining this independence is former Catalan Vice-President Josep-Lluís Carod-Rovira. A former political prisoner under General Franco's regime, Carod-Rovira became the president of the markedly separatist party of *Esquerra Republicana de Catalunya* (Republican Left of Catalonia). After the installation of the nationalist left-wing tripartite in 2003, Carod-Rovira became Catalonia's vice-president with a portfolio of diplomatic and foreign relations. Under his ministership, the erstwhile highly fragmented and dispersed diplomatic activities of the *Generalitat* underwent a process of streamlining, focus and professionalization. A broad national conversation was held on Catalonia's diplomatic priorities. Under the auspices of the *Patronat Catalunya Mon*, a private–public body representing both the *Generalitat* and the broader Catalan civil society, this national conversation resulted in the articulation of an ambitious foreign policy strategy. According to Carod-Rovira, this strategy was needed to strengthen further the region's diplomacy and nation-building policy, since 'Catalonia's world is the whole world. Catalonia has always viewed internationalization as an obligation and a responsibility, an opportunity and a mission, which cannot be avoided if we wish to exist, since we only exist in relation to others (Carod-Rovira 2010, 11)'.

One of the key instruments for achieving the goal of Catalan independence through a more robust diplomacy of its own is the opening of real Catalan embassies.[13] A very revealing text to gain more insight into the ideas of Carod-Rovira is the lecture that he gave at the London School of Economics in 2008 entitled 'The Role of Catalonia in Europe of the Twenty-first Century (Carod-Rovira 2009).' Transforming the stateless nation of Catalonia into a new European state of Catalonia is the main objective of the region's diplomatic activities, but this does not limit itself to Catalonia in *sensu stricto*, but also to the Catalan linguistic and cultural community:

> The European framework is meaningless without Catalonia, and Europe is not complete without Catalonia. [...] The Catalan culture, the Catalan linguistic space, includes part of the French state (northern Catalonia), a non-EU member (Andorra), the totality of Catalonia, Valencia and the Balearic islands, as well as a strip of territory in Aragon in the Spanish State, and an enclave on the Italian island of Sardinia (L'Alguer) (Ibidem).

The election in 2010, and even more so the re-election in 2012 of Artur Mas as Catalan president prompted a change in the guiding motive of Catalan paradiplomacy towards the international promotion of the process of

---

13 See, for example, '*Carod aprovecha reivindica en Israel la utilidad de las "embajadas" catalanas*', in: *El Mundo*, 17 November 2008; '*Diplomàcia catalane*', in *Directe!Cat*, 23 February 2011; and '*¿Y tu también, Cataluña?*', in: *El Mundo*, 27 July 2012.

self-determination.[14] During his presidency, a stark move towards political antagonism between Catalonia and Madrid occurred, as being highlighted in the organisation of the 2014 referendum on secession from Spain and the 2015 Catalan elections that were also presented and framed as a de facto referendum on Catalan independence. Catalan paradiplomacy has also undergone a sharp heterological shift. The erstwhile "double export" of economy and identity (Bizoux 2006) has gradually changed into a new double export of economy and the promotion of self-determination. Paradiplomacy in this regard became one of the key instruments in the Catalan governments' struggle for independence, which resulted in a steep rise in the Catalan budget allocated for its external activities, notably the opening of more foreign (pseudo-)embassies. As such paradiplomacy recently became an instrument of growing diplomatic heterology towards the central government in Madrid, as well as with the official Spanish diplomacy, by some labelled as a "diplomatic battle" between Barcelona and Madrid, with the *Generalitad* sending out delegations to national parliaments and to Washington to meet with U.S. congressmen, as well as writing official letters to foreign embassies defending the Catalan right to independence. At the same time Spanish Prime Minister Rajoy is seeking support with various European leaders, as well as with the European commission to defend Spain's right to full territorial integrity and unity. It remains to be seen how this tug of war will further develop, but one thing clearly stands out: Catalan diplomacy has embarked upon a path of unequivocal heterology vis-à-vis Madrid.

Quebec and Catalonia were not the only stateless nations to organize a referendum on more autonomy, or even downright independence. In September 18, 2014 the Scottish electorate was asked whether Scotland "should be an independent country". The referendum was, parallel to the Catalan case, instigated by the nationalists of the SNP who emerged as the largest party in the 2007 Scottish elections. Shortly after the election that resulted in the first minority SNP-led government then First Minister Alex Salmond launched the so-called "National Conversation", a public consultation on possible futures for the devolved government and governance, including the probability of an independence referendum. Contrary to Catalonia, the organization of the referendum, as well as its possible outcome was recognized beforehand by the British government. The referendum and the sometimes-fierce debates that surrounded it, have therefore at first glance, not turned into a site of political and diplomatic antagonism. However, on second look, there is an undeniable

14 For an analysis of the paradiplomatic activities of Catalonia under the presidency of Artur Mas, see: Ramón Lohmar Sainz de Vicuña, 2015.

spill over in the diplomatic realm of the dichotomy between the "Yes Scotland" and the "Better Together"-camps. Not only did Catalan and Basque politicians hail the referendum as a model for future referenda in their respective regions, thereby opposing the official Spanish reaction that stated that the Scots "have chosen the most favourable option for everyone; for themselves, for all of Britain and for the rest of Europe.[15]" A comparable variation was to be observed in the reaction of Quebec versus the response of Canada. There was a remarkable press release from the Russian ministry of foreign affairs, stating "It is an understandable and logical desire of the Scottish people for the central authorities to guarantee respect for their national and cultural identity, language and traditions and also give them more independence to take decisions on Scotland's socioeconomic development and its standing in the united state. We have noted that the UK government has extended concrete promises in this regard. We believe that these factors are extremely important not only for Scotland but also in the general context of devolution processes,[16]" a clear echo of the Russian support for Crimean and Eastern Ukrainian separatism. The referendum resulted in a 45% voting in favour of an independent Scotland. Yet the genie of political and diplomatic antagonism did not get into the bottle again. The United Kingdom general elections that occurred only half a year after the Scottish referendum, resulted in an electoral landslide, with the SNP winning 56 of 59 seats in Scotland, thereby affirming the strong position of Scottish nationalism.

Apart from organizing an independence referendum, the Scottish government is sometimes deliberately using its diplomatic activities to provoke the central state. Endowed with its own judicial system, the government of the devolved region took one of its most significant—and daring—diplomatic decisions in releasing the only man convicted of the bombing of the Pan-Am flight over Lockerbie. When Scottish Cabinet secretary for justice Kenny MacAskill announced the release of Abdelbaset Al-Megradhi in August 2009, his decision was met with either condemnation, distrust or a sense of disbelief. Some regarded the Scottish decision as a covert action of the British government to further its economic interests, and to facilitate the bilateral negotiations on illegal immigration and security issues, much against the will however of the United States. Libya on the other hand tried to better its negotiating position

15 "Scottish no vote best outcome for Europe, says Spanish PM Mariano Rajoy". Reuters. 19 September 2014.

16 "Comment by the Information and Press Department of the Russian Ministry of Foreign Affairs regarding the Scottish independence referendum". The Ministry of Foreign Affairs of the Russian Federation. 20 September 2014.

in the so-called scramble for Libya after the end of the international embargo. Daniel Kennealy offers an insightful account of the political and diplomatic triangulation between London, Edinburgh and Tripoli. He convincingly portrays the Scottish decision to release the bomber as a particular instance of highly politicized paradiplomacy, presenting it "in such a way to bolster the idea of Scotland as a distinct entity with its own set of values, laws, and customs and possessing an ability to operate autonomously on the international stage Kenealy 212, 555)." Political paradiplomacy, though its object in this case is of a humanitarian nature, is particularly "realist" in its aim to project itself externally to help advance its nation-building at home, by showing local leaders in international contexts (Keating 1999, 5).

2 *Counter- and Pseudo-embassies*

Another salient illustration of paradiplomacy as diplomatic heterology are the so-called "counter-embassies". These can literally take the form of embassies that are set up to go against the grain of the official embassies, but can also be foreign delegations of sub-state entities that have time and again been labeled embassies by friend and foe alike. The setting up of counter- (or pseudo-) embassies is part and parcel of paradiplomatic heterology in that these embassies are competing or conflicting with the state embassies they are positioned against. They moreover contest the international rules and norms on diplomatic representation, as they have developed since the Renaissance and that overtime have become a very subtle, balanced and sophisticated practice, in which reciprocity and mutual trust are paramount. In times of profound political crisis, such as secessionist struggle, civil war or ideological revolutions, the representational prerogatives of the old embassies are challenged and questioned by the new counter-embassies. Numerous examples of these instances of antagonistic paradiplomacy are to be found in the history of diplomacy, up to the present day. We will deal with one of the more telling historical examples, namely that of the Russian revolution. This is strictly speaking not a clear case of paradiplomacy as the diplomatic activities of sub-state political entities, but if we adhere to a more inclusive take on paradiplomacy, this can also become an instance of counter-diplomacy, when two competing political actors claim to represent the same territorial given (in this case Russia—the Soviet Union). We will also deal with the way in which the Belgian region of Flanders is setting up its own (pseudo-) embassies abroad, called the Flemish Houses.

One of the oldest examples of the counter-embassy, however, can be observed in the myriad of embassies and counter-embassies that existed in republican and imperial Rome, where at a certain time the Greek city of Sparta sent out four competing embassies, each of them representing another city quarter and/or another faction of the city (Brennan 2009, 186). Another more telling example is the revolutionary diplomacy of the early Soviet Union, which developed parallel to that of tsarist Russia, making it a particular site of historical paradiplomacy. From the outset, Bolshevist attitudes towards diplomacy were ambiguous, reflecting the various tendencies within the communist leadership and that between the two power-players in the definition and implementation of Soviet foreign policy: the *Comintern* (the Third Communist International) and the *Narkomindel* (ministry of foreign affairs). Both Lenin and Trotsky, who acted as the first Soviet foreign minister, were convinced of the necessity to get rid of the old diplomacy that was considered and portrayed as an instrument of both state-power and capitalist class dominance. International relations as they had been practiced and were still being practiced were regarded by the Soviet leadership as an instrument of the imperial(ist) regimes that had laid at the basis of the war and that had an interest in prolonging the war. The war was, according to Lenin *cum suis* a class war, designed by the European bourgeois elites to curtail the revolutionary socialist movements that had swept the continent in the last decade of the 19th century and the first decade of the 20th century. By incorporating the working class into a nationalist and territorial mass-frenzy, the European elites were able to divert them from an immanent class war.[17] To ensure class war, the early stages of Soviet foreign policy were primarily dictated by the needs of and designed by the people of the Third International. The *Comintern* was set up in Moscow in 1919 to fight "by all available means, including armed force, for the overthrow of the international bourgeoisie and for the creation of an international Soviet republic as a transition stage to the complete abolition of the State.[18]" Russian diplomacy, in the first months after the October Revolution, was primarily concerned with the disclosure of all the secret treaties and negotiations of the tsarist ministry of foreign affairs, as well as with issuing "a few revolutionary proclamations to the peoples of the world and then shut up shop (Carr 1985, 16)." To that end, early Soviet diplomacy explicitly countered traditional etiquette and protocol by abolishing diplomatic ranks, protocol and precedence rules or by stationing propagandists instead of professional diplomats abroad (Kocho-Williams 2012).

However, the harsh reality of the war made it hard for the Soviet leadership to maintain this revolutionary stance. Lenin willy-nilly had to accept the rules of the diplomatic game and was forced to postpone the coming into being of

17 For a refreshing Marxist interpretation of the First World War, see Pauwels 2014.

18 Minutes of the Third International, evening session of August 4, to consult on https://www.marxists.org/history/international/comintern/2nd-congress/ch10a.htm.

the world revolution. Moreover, Russian diplomats—whose allegiance still was to the tsarist regime—worldwide refused to accept the new political reality that was the Soviet-Union and the parallel revolutionary emissaries that were sent out by the Bolshevik leadership were arrested and deported in their respective host countries. It was therefore paramount at first to come to a swift cease-fire with Germany and the Habsburg Empire in order to consolidate the precarious political situation the Bolshevists faced in these early stages of the anti-communist counterrevolution.

The first site of official Soviet diplomacy is to be situated in the peace negotiations of Brest-Litovsk with representatives of the German empire in February 1918. These peace talks, apart from entailing the loss of a great deal of territory in return for an immediate cease-fire, implicitly entailed recognition of the new Soviet state and regime by the Germans, as well as of the new still hybrid diplomatic apparatus, including the new Soviet embassy in Berlin. This new counter-embassy was no ordinary embassy, but rather a revolutionary outpost in enemy territory, whose tasks were described by an American journalist living in Berlin as

> To neutralize the German generals, who wanted the Bolshevik Government removed (…). His second task was to assist revolutionary forces in Germany. The third was to collect intelligence on domestic conditions (Pipes 1991, 619).

This international legitimacy, albeit granted by an enemy power, was of the greatest importance for the at that time still very weak Russian revolutionaries, that had to deal with internal and external threats. It also offered the Soviets the "breathing spell" they needed to advance the revolution, attacked as it was on two fronts: on the one side by the still formidable German military machine and on the other side by the White counter-revolutionaries. The negotiations themselves proved to be one of the strangest sites of modern diplomacy, because,

> representatives of the most revolutionary régime ever known should sit at the same table with the representatives of the most reactionary military caste among the then ruling classes, that a Bavarian nobleman, a Knight of the Golden Fleece, and a Prussian major-general should negotiate on equal terms with a group of Bolshevik leaders but lately returned from exile, and from whose clothes the reek of dungeons had barely been banished (Wheeler-Bennet 1938, 1).

After Brest-Litovsk, the young revolutionary state increasingly gave up on establishing a new type of "revolutionary anti-bourgeois diplomacy", and tried to forge diplomatic ties with other countries in order to escape the diplomatic deadlock it had put itself in. This shift from the revolutionary foreign policy design of the *Comintern* to the pragmatic diplomatic practice of the *Narkomindel* was due to the unexpected and long political isolation of the young Soviet-Union. The support of successive proletarian revolutions in Central Europe did not materialize and this situation was likely to continue for the next few years at least (Jacobson 1994, 14). The years following Brest-Litovsk were therefore characterized by a gradual search for normalization and the quest for stable diplomatic relations. Simultaneously, it had become clear to both the United States and Western European powers that the Soviet Union was not going to collapse, as had been hoped, and that there was a very real need, at least on economic grounds, to engage with this new Russia. During the 1920s, an increasingly great number of European countries began to recognize the Soviet-Union, which resulted in the establishment of a network of Soviet embassies worldwide, the abolishment of the tsarist counter-embassies, as well as a growing number of foreign embassies in Moscow. This historical *entr'acte* illustrates the stark heterological dynamic that comes with political revolution and the establishment of counter-embassies.

Counter-embassies can also be of a less antagonistic, albeit still highly heterological nature. This is especially the case with the network of sub-state diplomatic representations that has sprawled during the last decades. One of the most telling examples is the Belgian region of Flanders that in two decades times has developed a dense network of diplomatic representations abroad. The emergence and development of Flemish (and indeed Walloon) paradiplomacy cannot be detached from the historical and political divide between the Dutch-speaking Northern part of Belgium and the French-speaking South (Wallonia). As such, the international policies of Flanders are to be seen as an emanation of "a particular type of regionalism, characterized by historical roots, strong identity, institutional opportunities and economic-financial performance (Delmartino 2011, 46)." From the outset, Flemish nationalism has been an important impetus for the genesis and development of Flanders' foreign policy.

From a diplomatic point of view, the Belgian case is a peculiar one, in that the Belgian regions (Flanders, Wallonia, Brussels and the German Community) do enjoy true diplomatic status thanks to the "*in foro interno, in foro externo*"—principle that is enshrined in the national constitution. According to this principle, the Belgian regions and communities are entitled to—and even obliged to—develop their international policies within their domestic policy domains. Consecutive state reforms have gradually increased the regions' policy portfolio at the detriment of the central state, including economy, labor, commerce, culture, education. This is a unique situation since

> In Belgium, the federal government cannot intrude in competences that belong to the constituent units. On the contrary, Belgian constituent units enjoy full legitimate and legal direct access to the international stage. This constitutional provision clearly goes beyond what can be found in other federal states (Bursens and Deforche 2010, 153).

Three immediate consequences derive from the "in foro interno, in foro externo"-principle. First, Flanders and Wallonia have the right to conclude international treaties with third parties, including states. Second, Flanders and Wallonia are also formally participating to the formulation of the Belgian foreign policy position (Criekemans 2010b, 6–7). Third, they have the right to send out diplomatic representatives, both bilateral and multilateral. Consecutive Flemish governments have forged a dense network of Flemish foreign delegations, surpassing more than a hundred political, economic, tourist, development and even agricultural representatives of the Flemish government, the most conspicuous being the political representations, labelled "representations of the Flemish government". The first of these representations was opened in Vienna in 1993, the year of the State Reform that enshrined the "in foro interno, in foro externo"-principle in the Belgian Constitution. The Austria delegation is also competent to represent Flanders in Hungary, the Czech Republic, Slovakia and Slovenia. Soon after came the so-called Flemish House in The Hague. The Netherlands can be considered one of the most important bilateral partners of the Flemish region, due to a myriad of historical, linguistic and economic linkages. Over the years the diplomatic network has come to include Paris, Berlin, London, Geneva, Brussels (EU), Pretoria, Madrid, Warsaw and New York. What is unique about these representatives of the Flemish government is that they have an official diplomatic statute, albeit a hybrid one. Constitutionally, they are an integral part of the Belgian diplomatic and consular representations abroad, and as such subject to the authority of the head of the mission. Functionally however, they are civil servants of the Flemish government, performing the tasks and directives assigned to them by their regional government (Velaers 2006, 44–35). This hybrid model is not without its tensions and frictions, as was the case in the 2009 controversy surrounding the Flanders House in New York, in which the Belgian minister of foreign affairs publicly shamed the Flemish government for opening such an expensive representation and its then director for fraud and embezzlement. The same Flanders

House caused a row in the Francophone press and with Francophone politicians when it organized a Dutch-Flemish cocktail evening, the invitation of which included a map situating Wallonia in France.

3 *Mimicry—Emulating the State*

Closely related to the logic of diplomatic antagonism and the instrument of pseudo-embassies is the practice of diplomacy as a site of political mimicry. Political mimicry is also an effect of with what Stéphane Paquin defines as 'identitary paradiplomacy', the international actorness of sub-state entities to access material and symbolic resources that they lack domestically, and to protodiplomacy, the diplomatic activities of regional authorities aimed at obtaining international recognition for their search for independence. Sub-state political authorities wanting to increase their domestic and international actorness, whether this actorness would result in full-fledged autonomy or not, are prone to emulate or mimic traditional diplomatic practices of the state. This process—whereby practices, discourses and symbols (such as the before mentioned pseudo-embassies) of traditional diplomacy are being copied by sub-state diplomatic actors—can be called 'diplomatic mimicry'. This is a global phenomenon, with certain sub-state entities making use of their diplomatic practices to promote a distinct nationalist, regionalist and/or separatist agenda. Quebec, the Basque Country, Scotland, Catalonia and Flanders try to emulate state diplomatic practices in order to appropriate this core element of 'stateness', thereby adding an extra layer to their already antagonistic practice of paradiplomacy.

An important theory of social and political mimicry was developed by René Girard in his seminal works Violence and the Sacred (Girard 1977). According to Girard, comprehending mimesis is inherently about understanding violence, competition, and adversity. It is not so much the value of the object that is desired—in this case, the diplomatic status and stature of the state as the most important international actor—but the fact that these very objects are the property of others or the target of other's desires. What is desired is thus the 'having' or the 'desiring' of the other. Desiring in the context of politics and diplomacy means wanting to appropriate the other's assets or desires; in other words, desiring in this context becomes a 'desire to being'. All desire is in fact desire to be (Girard 1996, 28).

Diplomatic stature, acknowledged in practice by the international community and codified in the various Vienna conventions on international and diplomatic relations, is desired by the diplomatic have-nots, which include certain sub-state entities. What they desire, however, according to the theory of mimetic desire, is not this mere stature or prerogative(s), but the fact that others desire or possess these prerogatives. What they desire is the 'Being' of the possessors—those that are in diplomatic relations—that is, the states to which they belong. Mimicry, according to Homi Bhabha, is a highly political activity. It is the appropriation of the Other as it visualizes power, via strategies of reform, regulation and discipline (Bhabha 1984, 126). While excluded from the traditional state system, which still remains the basis for international relations and the scholarly field of International Relations alike, the process of diplomatic mimicry by certain sub-state entities draws on the discourses and performances of 'traditional diplomats', deals with the political process on a global level, and still reifies the idea of international society (McConnell, Moreau and Dittmer 2012, 804). According to McConnell and others, the variety of mimicries available to sub-state diplomatic actors can vary, from loose mimicry that adopts some of diplomacy's customs and practices, to claims of diplomatic equivalence (McConnell, Moreau and Dittmer 2012, 806). Paradiplomacy, in this sense poses questions regarding legitimacy, sovereignty as well as recognition—in short, regarding diplomatic equivalence.

Practically all sub-state entities pursue at least a loose interpretation or adoption of certain diplomatic practices, whereby official state diplomatic practices are emulated or mimicked. The most conspicuous ones are the adoption of a state-like bureaucratic structure, including a pseudo-ministry of foreign affairs and the before mentioned network of pseudo-embassies. These can be of a very modest nature, as is the case with Northern or Eastern European sub-state entities, as well as certain Italian, French or Spanish regions. Take the Southern Italian region of Puglia, a lesser known but quite active paradiplomatic actor. Puglia's ministry of external relations, the *Servizio Mediterraneo*, is composed of fifteen staff members, while the region's foreign delegations include five civil servants (four in the Brussels office and one in the Tirana office). Also French Languedoc-Roussillon has a small *Direction des Relations Internationales et Union Européenne*, numbering fifteen staff members. On the other end of the spectrum, Catalonia's *Secretaria d'Afers Exteriors i de la Unió Europea* has more than 150 staff members, while its five *Delegacions del Govern de la Generalitat de Catalunya* house more than 25 staff members. The Canadian province of Quebec holds an impressive modular system of 7 general delegations (government offices), 4 delegations (government offices), 8 bureaus, 5 trade offices, as well as 2 areas of representation in multilateral affairs, while the Flanders Department of Foreign Affairs holds a network of ten diplomatic representations (called Flemish Houses), as well as a network of foreign trade and tourism offices.

Sub-state foreign offices are led by the representative abroad, who can be endowed with the title of 'Delegate of the Catalan Government' (Catalonia) or 'Delegate of the Junta of Andalusia', or merely as the 'Director of the

Office' (Puglia), or 'Director of the Representation of the region of Provence-Alpes-Côte d'Azur' or 'General Representative of the Government of Flanders' or 'Delegate General of Quebec'.

Within the paradiplomatic bureaucracies, there are often special units dealing with diplomatic protocol and ceremonial matters, making it a particular site for mimicry. *Le Protocole* is the administrative branch of the Quebec Ministry of Foreign Relations, responsible for application of the commitments made by Québec in international conventions and agreements relating to diplomats. It also deals with all matters regarding state ceremonial,[19] official missions abroad by the head of government, and official visits to the government. Next to this there is a *Direction du protocole et de l'accueil de l'Assemblée nationale*, whose mission is primarily concerned with Members of the National Assembly and is thus a highly formalized instance of parliamentary paradiplomacy. The *Service du Protocole* of the region of PACA and the *Direction des Relations Publiques et du Protocole of Languedoc-Roussillon* are part of the presidential cabinet, as are the *Servizio del protocollo* of Emilia-Romagna and the *Servizio Cerimoniale Eventi e Manifestazioni* of Puglia. The *Servicio de Protocolo de la Junta de Andalusia* is part of the *Consejeria Presidencia e Igualidad*, which also entails the external affairs department, as well as the Brussels office. The *Oficina de Protocol* of the Generalitat of Catalonia is part of the *Oficina del President I Coordinació Interdepartamental*, while the *Service des Relations Publiques et Protocole* of the Francophone part of Belgium is an integral part of the administrative branch of *Wallonie-Bruxelles International*. The importance that is placed on protocol by all of the sub-state entities is indicative of the mimetic desire, for 'although protocol is perhaps a soft issue, it still displays a willingness to be inclusive in high profile symbolic areas and a sign of the potential for change in diplomatic culture (Constantinou and Der Derian 2010, 12)'. The same logic of diplomatic mimicry can be observed in the importance that almost all sub-state entities place on high-level diplomatic visits, of which presidential visits are the most conspicuous. Marc Guerrero I Tarrago for instance has mapped the impressive list of presidential visits of former Catalan President Jordi Pujol (Guerrero i Tarrago 2007, 97). During his 23 years in office, Pujol made 378 presidential visits, 339 of which were in Europe, mainly in France (109) and Germany (61), but also fourteen to North

19 The Government of Quebec issued a number of decrees regarding diplomatic precedence, such as the "*Décret concernant l'ordre de préséance dans les ceremonies publiques*" (1990), as well as a highly detailed and formalized flag protocol, see: Displaying Flags and Symbols, online: http://www.mrif.gouv.qc.ca/en/protocole/pavoisement/pavoisement-drapeaux-emblemes.

America and eight to Latin America. Though certainly the most active foreign traveler, Pujol was and is far from the only regional president making ample use of this high-profile instrument. Indeed, foreign visits not only enhance the international and domestic stature of the region, they also raise the personal political profile of the president.

Not only regional presidents travel abroad to promote their region, also regional ministers as well as sub-state parliaments have increasingly made foreign diplomatic missions (Duran, Criekemans and Melissen 2008, 97). Stelios Stavridis has done quite some research on the role of regional parliaments in the construction and development of paradiplomacy, particularly in the Euro-Mediterranean space (Stavridis 2002 and Stavridis 2007). These parliamentary visits and exchanges are particularly poignant from the vantage point of diplomatic mimicry. Parliamentary diplomacy not only results in the internationalization of a specific polity, but also as legitimization of its sovereignty: it is not only the government that goes abroad, it is—according to Stavridis—the people via its elected parliamentary body. These parliamentary exchanges, both outgoing and incoming, can also become scenes of diplomatic heterology, political contestation or antagonism in which sub-state parliaments defy the diplomatic sensitivities of the central state they belong to. A notable and rather unexpected example is the way in which the regional assembly of the Italian region of Emilia-Romagna deals with representatives from Western Sahara. Emilia-Romagna is one of the most supportive governments for the Sahrawi case, which has translated itself into an annual increase in funding and activities since 1999. The regional government of Emilia-Romagna, which has always had a markedly left-wing character, actively develops diplomatic ties with the Polisario government, as is illustrated by the 2011 encounters of the former President of Emilia-Romagna's Regional Assembly, Matteo Richetti, with SADR (Sahrawi Arab Democratic Republic) Prime Minister Abdelkader Taleb Omar and the Polisario's representative in Italy, Omar Mih, during which Richetti repeatedly stressed Emilia-Romagna's dedication to a peaceful solution and freedom for Western Sahara's people. These diplomatic ties go back to the 1990s and since then Emilia-Romagna has organized multiple official visits and signed various protocols of intent with representatives of SADR. Moreover, representatives of the Emilia-Romagnan government have repeatedly and publicly expressed their support for the Polisario case, thus transgressing the official diplomatic position of Italy, which does not recognize the Sahrawi Arab Democratic Republic (Fresa 2006, 167). Representatives of the Polisario Front, but also of the Tibetan government-in-exile, the Kurdish Democratic Party and other controversial and contested diplomatic interlocutors, have been in direct diplomatic contact with parliamentary assemblies in Spanish Catalonia and Andalusia, as well as Italian Puglia and Emilia-Romagna.

Once again (and in line with the logic of political and diplomatic antagonism), Catalonia stands out as the archetypical example of this specific mimetic dynamic in paradiplomacy. Its political and historical position as a historic nation within the Spanish state, as well as its current situation of stateless nation within Europe, accentuates its nationhood, albeit one that is not recognized by the Spanish state configuration nor by the European regional policies, or by its international interlocutors. Catalan nationalism being widespread among the Catalan population, results in a relative consensus about Catalonia's international strategy, including the diplomatic priorities of the *Generalitat*. The Catalan government therefore formulates and practices a diplomacy that can only be described as far-reaching in its mimicry of state diplomacy. Emphasizing international representation and diplomatic protocol, adhering to international organizations such as the different UN bodies, adopting a sometimes antithetic discourse, allocating impressive budgets for its international and developmental policies, Catalonia is positioning itself on the world map as part of the international community, or in the words of former Catalan President and the prime architect of Catalan diplomacy Jordi Pujol, '*El nostre món es el Món, més que mai*' (Our world is the World, more than ever), thereby highlighting the importance of Catalonia on the world stage and its urgency, its desire, to be a full-fledged actor on this world stage. The Catalan *Generalitat* therefore appropriates symbols of diplomatic legitimacy in order to maintain its governmental claims, including the language of 'stateness.' (Hansen and Stepputat 2001, 9).

Political antagonism, the establishment of counter-embassies and the development of a diplomatic practice that closely resembles that of the (traditional) state are to be found on the "heterology"-end of the diplomatic continuum that is the separation dynamics. They are designed and carried out to enhance political differences and diplomatic dissimilarities, mainly in opposition to the central state certain sub-states, with a strong nationalist heritage or tradition belong to.

Homology

At the other end of the spectrum, in opposition to diplomatic mimicry, another form of inter-polity relationships can be observed, a relationship that centres on the human and humanistic aspects of diplomacy. Coined as homo-diplomacy by Costas Constantinou because of its double genealogic—etymologic origin, as (1) stressing the commonalities instead of the degrees of separation (*homoios*: the same, relating), or (2) the human, day-to-day aspects of diplomacy (*homo*: man, human). Homo- or human diplomacy implies a true paradiplomacy; it holds the potential for a distinctly different kind of diplomacy, transgressing the boundaries of diplomacy, which still limits the practice of sub-state diplomacy. This article believes that by adhering to human diplomacy, sub-state entities can find a way to break out of the deadlock into which they manoeuvred themselves by desiring to be 'as state-like as possible' while not being able to be states. It is important to stress that human diplomacy is being practised or can be practised by all human groupings or individuals, including states and mimicking sub-state entities. Even the 'most mimicking' sub-state entities, Catalonia, Flanders and Quebec are in some respects practising a form of human diplomacy.

An archetypical example of the dynamics of paradiplomatic homo-diplomacy was delivered by the then regional representative of the Italian region of Emilia-Romagna in Jerusalem. When he visited Israel in February 2010, Italian Prime Minister Silvio Berlusconi not only put forward the possibility of future EU membership for Israel, but also called upon the Palestinians to recognize Israel. His remarks caused anger among Hamas and the population of Gaza at large. Residences and cars of Italian and other European officials were vandalized and tensions mounted between Palestinians and Italian NGOs operating in the region. To decrease the tensions, the representative of the Italian region of Emilia-Romagna and a local imam in East Jerusalem drafted a joint proclamation, in which they stressed the good intentions of both parties in the name of common interests and a shared Mediterranean humanity, which must not be jeopardized by the reckless statements of state officials. Slowly, the cutting of tyres and the smashing of windows stopped, and, what was more, the shared declaration formed the basis for intensified cooperation by Emilia-Romagna's NGOs (at the time the only Italian region left in Gaza) and local Hamas officials. Emilia-Romagna at the same time tried to facilitate contacts between the Israeli Defence Forces (IDF) and local Palestinian authorities in order to enable joint Israeli–Palestinian projects, such as bringing together, in shared 'mourning gatherings', Palestinian and Israeli children and adults who have lost relatives during the second Intifada (Regione Emilia-Romagna 2010, 177–181). Since then, all Italian regions have left Israel/Palestine, and this episode of 2010 risks of becoming just a past memory. However, this concern about bringing together and even mediating between antagonists in war-torn countries can also be found in Emilia-Romagna's attempts to develop Moroccan–Sahrawi encounters, both in Western Sahara and in the Polisario refugee camps in

Algeria. These social, educational, and logistic projects are intended to enforce Sahrawi culture, as well as to look for common ground with local Moroccan authorities, often in cooperation with the Red Crescent.

By engaging in peace building and peace politics, sub-state entities engage in accommodating social, cultural and humanist similarities, and overcome the oppositional logic that often comes with international relations. In doing so, they practice a mature form of diplomacy, aimed at harmonizing conflicting principles and ideas. The same dynamic is to be found in the particular model of decentralized development cooperation projects and programs that are being set up by sub-state entities. This model surpasses the traditional asymmetric donor-recipient dynamic and replaces it with a governance model based on equity between two diplomatic partners.

1 *Peace Building—Peace Politics*

Emilia-Romagna is certainly not the only regional entity practicing homodiplomacy, far from it. Other regions, such as Quebec, Catalonia, and Flanders, but also lesser known regional entities, such as Languedoc-Roussillon and Provence-Alpes-Côte d'Azur acknowledge the need to broker between Israel and Palestine, or between Morocco and Western Sahara or engage in other humanist diplomatic activities.

Some sub-state governments are even more ambitious and want to take an active role in peace-building and conflict prevention. The surge in the concept and practice of peace-building occurred during the early 1990s, at about the same time as the advent of paradiplomacy as a foreign policy practice, particularly after the publication of the report by then secretary-general of the UN, Boutros Boutros-Ghali "An agenda for peace: preventative diplomacy, peacemaking and peacekeeping".[20] The first Gulf War, as well as the violent dissolution of the Soviet Union and Yugoslavia put the management of international as well as internal conflicts high on the agenda. According to Didier Verbruggen, it is important to differentiate between peace-building, conflict prevention and development cooperation or humanitarian aid. This differentiation enables us to consider peace policies as pillars of a broader foreign policy and, especially for a sub-state entity, as a means to put oneself in the spotlight as a responsible international player and as a 'peace-broker' (Verbruggen 2015, 15–17). Both Catalonia and Flanders figure as two of the most

20 United Nations, *An Agenda for Peace. Preventive diplomacy, peacemaking and peacekeeping, Report of the Secretary- General pursuant to the statement adopted by the Summit Meeting of the Security Council on 31 January 1992*, A/47/277—S/24111, 17 June, http://www.unrol.org/files/A_47_277.pdf.

prolific paradiplomatic 'peace-brokers', thereby encompassing both ends of the heterological-homological continuum.

Both in its international policy strategy and in its constitutional status the Catalan *Generalitat* mentions its ambition to contribute to international conflict prevention and peace-building. Especially the advent of the centre-left tripartite government in 2003 signified an important impetus for the development and institutionalization of an already strong and vibrant Catalan peace movement. The adoption of the Peace Promotion Act by the Catalan Parliament on 4 July 2003 signified the beginning of the establishment of a series of activities as well as governmental bodies for peace-building and conflict prevention. With this aim, both an administration, the *Consell Català de Foment de la Pau*, and an institution, the International Catalan Institute for Peace were established within the Catalan Parliament. The Institute for Peace conducts work and study in the fields of human security, conflict management and conflict prevention, peace-building and the protection of human rights. In addition to organizing workshops, training courses for foreign diplomats and publishing policy reports and legal papers, the Institute has accomplished a number of missions in Ivory Coast, Colombia, Mexico and Bolivia since its beginning in 2007. Observing elections and post-election monitoring of the democratization process and strengthening the rule of law, as well as guiding legal transition processes, were paramount during these missions. Peace promotion is also part and parcel of Catalonia's system of development cooperation, with a special focus on capacity building, peace mediation and dialogue, especially aimed at Columbia and the Western Sahara.

We can detect a comparable pattern in Flanders, a region that has, due to its historical legacy, an experienced peace movement and a strong tradition in remembering and promoting peace, notably since the Flemish national movement went hand in hand with the peace movement after the First World War (Van Alstein 2011). One of the first comprehensive foreign policy programs of the Flemish government comprised an important peace building and peace promotion part. As already mentioned, Flemish diplomacy really took off at the same time when the countries of Eastern and Central Europe cast off the communist regime and began their transition towards Western capitalism and parliamentary democracy. The Flemish government initiated the "Central and Eastern Europe Program", aimed at assisting these countries fulfil the traditional pre-accession conditions regarding peace-building in the areas of human rights, good governance and democratisation. Also during the 1990s did the Flemish government organize a summer school for adolescents in conflict or post-conflict areas, such as Abkhaziä, Israel-Palestine, Nagorno-Karabakh, as well as Northern Ireland. Recently, the Flemish government is developing a specific policy on human rights, until now a prerogative of the federal ministry of foreign affairs, a situation that is, in the words of Flemish prime minister and minister of foreign affairs, "not tenable any more," since "the regions have to be actively involved in the formulation and implementation of a human rights policy. This should be an inter-federal competence.[21]"

After the regionalisation of the Belgian arms trade in 2003, the Flemish government decided to establish a "Flemish Peace Institute" within the regional parliament, "to conduct scientific research on peace issues and offer its findings to support the activities of the Flemish Parliament. The Institute provides information and documentation and makes recommendations to the Parliament.

Its documents address issues that are relevant for not only policymakers but also civil society organisations and the public at large.[22]" Two research lines are developed within the Flemish Peace Institute, one on arms trade and arms production, and one on peace and society. The Flemish Peace Institute is also one of the paramount actors in the establishment of the Trauma and Transformation Network (TTN). This TTN was meant to bundle all Flemish expertise in trauma treatment and societal transformations. In the words of then Flemish prime minister Kris Peeters: "Within the frame of this network, we will initially gather all Flemish expertise and scientific knowledge regarding trauma treatment and the transformation of societies. In the long term, the TTN will be a flexible and targeted policy instrument that can rapidly and globally be deployed in certain areas or circumstances. This can happen at the request of a foreign partner, or on our own initiative.[23]" The genesis of the TTN coincided with the ambitions to put Flanders on the international map as a reliable peace-broker and peace partner during the built up to and the actual commemoration of the First World War centennial.

There are also lesser known, less institutionalized but evenly active regions involved in peace promotion and peace policy. Particularly in the Mediterranean region, we can see this homodiplomatic logic at work, the region being the meeting place (or fracture point, or battle field, depending of the vantage point one holds) between three continents, three religions and various political and economic systems. An important tool for Mediterranean

21 Geert Bourgeois, Answer to parliamentary question number 2601 (2014–2015) in the Flemish parliament, July 7, 2015.

22 Taken from the website of the Flemish Peace Institute: http://www.vlaamsvredesinstituut.eu/sites/vlaamsvredesinstituut.eu/files/wysiwyg/vvi_web_algemene voorstellingsbrochure_en.pdf.

23 Cited by Didier Verbruggen, *Vredesopbouw en conflictpreventie*, 9.

sub-state entities to achieve this goal is the historical remembrance within the Mediterranean. The capital of the French region of Languedoc-Roussillon, Montpellier, for instance, hosts the Euro-Mediterranean research university *Institut Maïmonide*, which was co-founded by Georges Frêche, the late president of the region of Languedoc-Roussillon, and Chief Rabbi René-Samuel Sirat. The Institute, which is housed in Montpellier's medieval *Mikvé* (or bath house) is a place for scholarly, cultural and other encounters on the themes of Jewish, Christian and Muslim life in the Mediterranean, yesterday and today. Not only the historical places of peaceful cohabitation and encounters, but also the darker places of memory play a role in Mediterranean homodiplomacy. During the Second World War, one of the biggest massacres in Italy occurred near Bologna. This so-called 'Marzabotto Massacre' now serves as the foundation of an Italian–German Peace School of Monte Sole, where annual peace camps are held that bring together children from Israel and Palestine, Italy and Germany, and Kosovo and Serbia.

2 *Development Cooperation*

Particularly in the area of development cooperation important steps were and are made by sub-state entities, to advance their own diplomatic priorities and foreign policy, since cooperation assistance is a central argument used by regional officials to justify the existence of paradiplomacy (Lecours 2008, 5). Sub-state development cooperation increasingly assents to the 'New Aid Approach', whose basic principles are mutual partnership, local ownership, empowerment, participation and a long-term development practice (Waeterloos 2008, 6). "New Aid"-development cooperation shifts foreign aid away from the previous uneven relationship between a donor and a receiver towards a more diplomatic relationship between equal partners. Foreign aid, in this sense, is about the relationship between governmental and non-governmental actors and not about patterns of dependency (Lancaster 2007, 13). Sub-state entities have increasingly developed a cooperation model of multi-stakeholder policy, whereby the regional government cooperates with, oversees and assists other local authorities (provinces, cities and municipalities), non-governmental organizations and private bodies that are active in the sphere of development cooperation.

In a number of countries, such as Germany, the United Kingdom, Belgium, Spain, but also in Italy and France, local and regional governments are responsible for the conduct of large portions of development cooperation and have increasingly gained substantial degrees of freedom to set their own priorities in the realm of foreign aid. Unexpectedly, one of the most prolific examples are Italian regions, that have been experimenting with a particular model of multilevel and multi-actor decentralized cooperation. Since the beginning of the 1990s, Italian local authorities—whether regions, provinces or municipalities—have all made their first steps in the field of decentralized development cooperation (Stocchiero 2007, 5). In 2001, the organization of the Directorate-General for Development Cooperation of the Italian Ministry of Foreign Affairs was reformed so that local authorities could take more initiatives. This only met an already existing reality, in which several Italian regions were very active in establishing projects in the realm of development cooperation, especially aimed at Latin America, the Maghreb and the Middle East. Based on a number of normative principles, such as respect for local development, sustainability, decentralization and empowerment, Italian decentralized development cooperation has seen a significant increase in funding by the local authorities since 2000. The region of Emilia-Romagna has over the years been one of the country's most prolific players in the field of substate development cooperation. Its NGOs, provinces and municipalities have a long-standing tradition and their work is coordinated within the so-called Country Tables, which group all concerned actors that are active within a specific receiving country. The key priorities for Emilia-Romagna's foreign aid are in effect long-term interventions, sustainable and humanitarian actions, participatory development and the principle of reciprocity. Over time, the region has developed a model of multi-stakeholder policy, whereby the regional government cooperates with, oversees and assists other local authorities, nongovernmental organizations and private bodies that are active in the sphere of development cooperation. Emilia-Romagna's foreign aid aims at making a difference with traditional 'bilateral state development cooperation'. This can even be traced in the tagline of the platform for the region's development cooperation: 'Development cooperation—International relations between peoples—Promotion of a culture of peace'. The region's development cooperation is a good example of a multi-level policy based on the principles of subsidiarity: it operates in coordination and cooperation with the Italian Ministry of Foreign Affairs, the provinces and communities, other public entities such as ERVET, the economic development agency of the region, universities and the civil society.

Emilia-Romagna targets a limited number of countries for its development cooperation, clustered in four geographic areas: Africa; Latin America; the Balkans; and the Middle East. Special attention is given to developing countries, newly industrialized countries and pre-EU accession countries, via the Integrated Area Programmes. These programmes partly overlap with the region's decentralized cooperation schemes and target the western Balkans,[24]

24 Serbia, Montenegro, Albania, Bosnia-Herzegovina and Kosovo.

Eastern European countries,[25] Mediterranean countries,[26] sub-Saharan Africa;[27] Latin America;[28] and China and India.

Contrary to other countries, where the economic crisis resulted in substantial budget cuts in the field of decentralized cooperation; Italian development aid witnessed a transfer from the central government to the regional authorities. As a result, regional authorities—in cooperation with local NGOs and local small and medium enterprises—are becoming the main actors of Italy's development aid. Also in the southern Italian region of Puglia, foreign aid policy shifted to the new foreign aid paradigm, emphasizing the importance of peace promotion, poverty reduction and human rights. The guiding principles of Puglia's regional framework on decentralized cooperation are partnership, reciprocated development, multi-actorness and multi-level cooperation, democratic ownership, subsidiarity, mutual responsibility and mutual accountability, and sustainability. Puglia seeks to situate itself in the centre of a multi-actor system of foreign aid, amid the local authorities (provinces and communes), the national level, and NGOs. The region's decentralized cooperation is put into practice in five *Accordi di Programma Quadro* (APQs, or so-called programme agreement frameworks): the APQ Mediterranean; the APQ Balkans; '*Legge 84*'; '*Minori in Albania*'; and FOSEL.[29] Morocco, Tunisia, Algeria, Egypt and Jordan are the main receivers of these strands of foreign aid. Of particular interest is the so-called *Minori in Albania* (Minors on Albania)-program, aimed at integrating Albanian minors, both at home and in Italian society.

Also France has turned, quite remarkably, into a country with an unique system of decentralized development cooperation. After the implementation of the French decentralization laws of 1982, regional and departmental development cooperation rapidly increased. A number of legal and institutional modifications have since broadened the scope for 'decentralized cooperation of territorial collectivities'. The first was the Law on Decentralized Cooperation

25 Belarus, Ukraine and Moldova.

26 Morocco, Lebanon, Palestine and the Sahrawi Arab Democratic Republic.

27 Eritrea, Ethiopia, Mozambique and Senegal.

28 Brazil, Argentina and Cuba.

29 Apart from FOSEL, which is a training programme for local economic development in Argentina, the four other APQs are targeting the Mediterranean region, with considerable emphasis on the larger Balkan area. The APQ Mediterranean consists of five macro-thematic lines of action in the field of socio-economic development, education and logistics (the so-called 'interconnectivity between the material and the immaterial'), environment and sustainable development, dialogue and culture, and health and welfare.

of 6 February 1992, which opened the way for French regions, departments and municipalities to develop their own foreign aid.[30]

The southern French region of Provence-Alpes-Cote d'Azur was one of the pace-setters in this process. Already in 1979, it was the first French region to enter into decentralized cooperation, when it signed its first cooperation treaty with the *willaya* of Algiers. In 1984, Provence-Alpes-Cote d'Azur established its first decentralized cooperation programme, even before this was regulated by law, mainly in the domains of cultural cooperation, education, sustainable development and economic development. Within Provence-Alpes-Cote d'Azur, the International Humanitarian Mission mobilizes local authorities, NGOs and private institutions that are active in the region's development cooperation, mainly in North Africa. The economic crisis and the Arab Spring, however, have altered the context of French cooperation in the Mediterranean, both centralized and decentralized. The emphasis of Languedoc-Roussillon's decentralized cooperation also lies on Africa[31] and the greater Mediterranean region,[32] with cooperation agreements on education, sustainable (agricultural) development and culture. (Higher) education seems an especially important platform for Languedoc- Roussillon's decentralized cooperation, as well as its diplomatic contacts. Since the region wants to highlight its preponderance as a territorial benchmark in all matters research and development, its diplomatic activities also rely on the region's educational policy. Languedoc-Roussillon is therefore an important partner in the student exchange programme Averroès, which brings together students from southern France, Algeria, Morocco and Tunisia.

Spanish autonomous communities enjoy more freedom than French or Italian regions to establish their own foreign aid, which is legally set out in the various statutes. In Catalonia for instance, article 51 of the Statute states that: '(1). The *Generalitat* shall promote a culture of peace and actions that foster peace in the world. (2) The *Generalitat* shall promote cooperation actions and policies for the development of peoples and shall establish emergency humanitarian aid programmes', while article 197.3 affirms that 'the *Generalitat* shall promote development cooperation programmes'. Likewise, the Statute of Andalusia lists international cooperation with the objective of contributing to

30 In the first decade of the twenty-first century, the Oudin–Santini Law (2005), the Pintat Law (2006) and the Thiollière Law (2007) laid the foundations for, respectively, foreign aid in gas and electricity matters, the financing of decentralized cooperation, and the possibility to sign international agreements regarding decentralized cooperation.

31 Benin, Burkina-Faso, Kenya, Niger and Senegal.

32 Tunisia, Morocco, Algeria and Palestine.

the solidarity and development of the peoples as one of the basic policy objectives of the autonomous community. The guiding principles of Andalusia's development cooperation are poverty reduction, democratization, human rights and peace promotion, while its geographical focus is the Maghreb, Africa and Latin America. The *Agència Catalana de Cooperació al Desanvolupament* (ACCD, Catalan Agency for Development Cooperation) was established in 2003 in order to coordinate the already existing Catalan cooperation programmes. It is responsible for the region's development cooperation, including peace-building policies and humanitarian aid. Catalonia has elaborated a triple-action spherical scheme, whereby the work of the ACCD is divided into four geographic spheres, namely the Mediterranean, sub-Saharan Africa, Central America (including the Caribbean) and South America. In addition, Catalonia has selected eleven priority countries and peoples.

The activities of the ACCD have increased significantly since the advent of the centre-left tripartite in 2003 and aims at enhancing the role of Catalonia's public and private players. Until 2011, not only did the scope of Catalan foreign aid increase, but also its annual budget. The reason for this is twofold: on the one hand, the coming into power of the tripartite socialist-nationalist-green government marked a political swing to the left, as a result of which the ideas of the broader civil society on development cooperation were taken into more account; and on the other hand, the more outspoken nationalist government used the platform of decentralized cooperation to pursue its multilateral diplomatic ambitions. However, the sovereign debt crisis put a sudden halt to the steady increase of Catalan development cooperation. Not only did the ACCD's budget drop by almost 50 per cent in 2011–2012, the Catalan government also failed to follow up on its agreements with a substantial number of Catalan NGOs that are engaged in foreign aid.[33]

The Southern region of Andalusia's foreign aid is carried out by the governmental Andalusian Agency for International Development Cooperation (AACID), which was founded in 2008. This organization is responsible for the implementation of the Andalusian plan of development cooperation, which in accordance with the Statute lists the functional and geographic priorities. As with the case of Catalonia's decentralized cooperation, the left-wing political reality of Andalusia is beneficial to the ideological foundations of its foreign aid, which are codified in the Andalusian Pact for Solidarity. These principles are in line with the Millennium Goals of the United Nations, as well as with the Paris Declaration, and include protection of the environment and sustainable development, gender equality, cultural diversity, and an increased role for civil society. From these general principles stem the concrete

33 Adeu, cooperació!', in: El Pais, 26 July 2012.

operationalization of Andalusia's development cooperation. First, this means generating development processes in the region's priority spheres—that is, North Africa and the Middle East, sub-Saharan Africa and Latin America—consolidation of the region's humanitarian activities, development education for the Andalusian population, and strengthening the capacities of Andalusian development-cooperation actors. Analogous to the Catalan model, Andalusia has chosen a number of priority countries, of which four are situated in the Mediterranean region: Morocco; Western Sahara; Palestine; and Mauretania. The AACID also coordinates initiatives in the field of foreign aid of the region's local authorities, as well as its broader civil society and its network of NGOs (Izzo 2006, 25–26).

There are, next to peace policies and development cooperation other instances of humanist diplomacy, such as education cooperation, bringing together scholars and students in new scholarly and academic communities.

Especially in Europe, this has created a large interregional and cross-border community of scholars and students of universities and other institutions of higher education throughout the European Union. The advent of the modern state and its borders thwarted the international mobility of students and professors, but different European exchange programmes, such as Erasmus, have softened these academic borders. Both the Euro-Mediterranean University in Piran (Slovenia) and the Eurocampus of the Pyrenees-Mediterranean Euregion, which brings together more than half a million students and 45,000 researchers from the universities of Languedoc-Roussillon, Midi-Pyrénées, Catalonia, Aragon and the Balearic Islands, are new crossroads for intellectual but also human encounters in the region. Other notable examples are the Dutch-Flemish University of Hasselt-Maastricht, or the French-Walloon-Flemish university community of Lille-Kortrijk-Louvain-la-Neuve.

Cross-border educational cooperation, resulting in a new, albeit still embryonic, European academic community, a new more equal model of development cooperation, as well as the various peace building efforts of sub-state entities highlight the homology-end of the diplomatic continuum. Political, cultural and economic differences are being replaced by a clear desire to engage in common projects, in common interest and to emphasise the shared humanity of all the diplomatic protagonists and antagonists.

Conclusion and Possible Implications

After this brief overview of various sites of both heterological and homological patterns in paradiplomacy, we must return to the initial question: does this combination of realist power play and humanist policies of sameness signal the coming of age of paradiplomacy? Do these sites deliver enough evidence of an international political practice that has gained the necessary maturity to truly engage with the outside world? During its infant years, paradiplomacy often displayed a limited scope with regards to its functional or geographical priorities. It could the result and/or the catalyst of political antagonism (Catalonia and Quebec), of a complex state structure (the Belgian regions), of a functionalist division of labor (France and Italy), sometimes even of an EU-promoted model of multilevel governance (the Bulgarian *oblasts*). As a result practitioners of paradiplomacy initially limited themselves often to a one-dimensional either/or approach towards their diplomatic activities. In the absence of important political animosities with the central government, or as a result of their narrow constitutional bandwidth, some sub-state entities concentrated themselves on a mainly humanist set of policies. Notable examples hereof are the ways in which French and Italian regions developed their own system of decentralized development cooperation, turning it into various sites of multilayered encounters of local authorities, NGO's, companies and individuals. Others have, due to their strained relations with the central state developed a more politicized model of paradiplomacy, in which diplomatic actions and discourses are designed to accentuate the heterology with the central state or other sub-state entities.

Over the years, however, paradiplomacy has become more differentiated, each paradiplomatic actor displaying a more stratified, more inclusive blueprint for its international activities. So is Catalonia putting itself on the international map as a credible peace-broker, while Emilia-Romagna is using its peace policies as a means to set itself apart from the central Italian government, sometimes even going diametrically against the grain of the official foreign policy. Over the years, and as a result of its governmental middle ground positioning, paradiplomacy often became to hold an intermediate position between realist power play and humanist diplomacy. Sub-state entities do defend the interests of (the inhabitants of) their territory and its socio-economic positioning in the contemporary globalized configuration, and as such compete with other sub-state entities and other internationally active political actors. On the other hand, they often strengthen—both in practice and in discourse—political, cultural, social and economic ties with other sub-state entities and with other internationally active actors. As a result of their specific political gravity, they also function as pivots of various instances of homologic diplomacy, functioning as a mediator between different peoples. The role of the Spanish Autonomous Community of Catalonia in the emergence of various Euro-Mediterranean policies—whereby the Catalan *Generalitat* acts as a go-between, linking the European Union, the Spanish state and numerous NGOs, universities, cultural actors and corporations on both sides of the Mediterranean Sea—is a textbook example of this mediating role of paradiplomacy.

However, in times of heightened political tensions, of economic insecurity, budgetary austerity, and security crises, the relevance of paradiplomacy might be put in question. Can our current world still afford the existence of such diplomatic frivolities, while governments worldwide face all sorts of dangers and challenges? Wouldn't it be wiser to let the "big boys", the states play the game of diplomacy, instead of the myriad of "small boys", such as local authorities, NGO's or indeed sub-state political entities? Wouldn't it be more sane, just from a budgetary point of view, to get rid of all these parallel little diplomatic actors, each with their own mini-ministry of foreign affairs, their own network of pseudo- or even counter-embassies, their own desire to gain international stature and personality? More, is paradiplomacy not one of the elements that make our world in turmoil even more uncertain? Do the cases of Catalonia and Scotland not prove that paradiplomacy is an instrument in the hands of political actors wishing to rip apart countries and societies? Or does paradiplomacy not risk to become an instrument in the hands of third parties in their quest for destabilization of their enemies, as is the case with Russian-backed paradiplomacy in the Russian "near-abroad" of Gagauzia and Moldova (Cantir 2015)?

At first glance and intuitively, it would be quite possible to answer in the affirmative to this set of questions. Yet, conceding to this call to let diplomacy once again only be acted out by the traditional players, might result in an impoverishment of the separation dynamics. From a domestic point of view, it might seem a tempting idea to simply shut down the difficulties that come with political antagonism by silencing the contesting voices that arise from the heterological paradiplomacy. However, closing counter- and pseudo-embassies, prohibiting autonomy referenda or constitutionally and budgetary curtailing sub-state entities' possibilities to engage with the outside world, does not make way with the underlying political problems and societal tensions. This line of thought and of conduct would only perpetuate and even heighten the dynamic of political discord, making paradiplomacy a weapon in a political feud between the state and the sub-state. Instead of resorting to these in essence Hegelian or Marxist conceptualizations of political conflict and antagonisms, it would be better to consider paradiplomacy as a site of political agonism. Agonism emphasizes the inevitability—as well as the positive aspects—of political conflict. Agonism or agonistic pluralism, as it is sometimes labelled, offers a consistent model for thinking about so-called diplomatic Other-ing as a constitutive element of a political self-construction and dealing with separateness (Cornago 2013, 75). Indeed, Chantal Mouffe argues that:

> Once we understand that every identity is relational and that the affirmation of a difference is a precondition for the existence of any identify—i.e. the preconception of something 'other' which constitutes its 'exterior'—we can understand why politics, which always deals with collective identities, is about the constitution of a 'we' which requires as its very condition of possibility the demarcation of the 'they' (Mouffe 2013, 5).

Thus considered, paradiplomacy becomes a means to channel, to discuss and debate, in other words to mediate the various degrees of separateness between the state and its constitutive units.

From an international vantage point, it would be evenly wrong to silence the diplomatic voices of non-state actors, including sub-state political entities. Instead, an integrative or mega- (cfr. Parag Khanna) model of diplomacy, taking all relevant diplomatic players on board is more apt to deal with the growing complexities of today's world. This integrative model raises a number of questions that are formulated by Paul Sharp, Jan Melissen, Brian Hocking and Shaun Riordan:

> If the key characteristic of diplomacy in the 21st century is the emergence of multiactor networks, what demands does this place on the participants within them? One of the key challenges confronting both the structures and processes of diplomacy is the need to work with 'coalitions of the willing'. How can these be constructed and managed? How can the qualities of the broad range of 'stakeholders' with whom professional diplomats now need to operate be determined and leveraged for the delivery of policy objectives? (Hocking et al. 2013, 13)

Coordinating these 'coalitions of the willing', ad-hoc or more structural multiactor networks, is indeed the essence of diplomatic mediating, not only between various diplomatic actors, such as states and sub-state entities, but also between the principles, the ideas of heterology and homology.

Looking at paradiplomacy as a particular site of dealing with political separation and estrangement also enables the formulation of a possible future research agenda. A further inquiry into the interplay, both politically and diplomatically, between the various diplomatic antagonists of the separation dynamic would be beneficial for the refining and deepening of what is still a tentative analytical model for the further study of paradiplomacy. Particularly the relations between the different governance levels need to be further investigated to get a better insight into the multi-level and multi-actor dynamics between on the one hand the state, and on the other hand all the higher- and lower tier governance levels, including the European Union (in particular the European External Action Service, as well as the various European Neighbourhood Policies), sub-state entities and cities. This would also include the mapping of the multitude of diplomatic links, networks and grids that have gone to encompass our current global setting. This would come down to charting a map of the territory of political and diplomatic relations that could guide both scholars and practitioners into the myriad of engagements and commonalities, programs and projects, animosities and antagonisms.

References

Acuto, Michele. 2013. *Global cities, governance and diplomacy: The urban link.* Oxford: Routledge.

Adler-Nissen, Rebecca. 2015. "Just Greasing the Wheels? Mediating Difference or the Evasion of Power and Responsibility in Diplomacy." *The Hague Journal of Diplomacy* 10: 22–28.

Banai, Husein. 2014. "Diplomatic imaginations: mediating estrangement in world society." Cambridge Review of International Affairs 27/3: 459–474.

Bélanger, Luis. 1997. "Les enjeux actuels de la participation du Québec à la francophonie multilatérale: de la paradiplomatie à la protodiplomatie." *Politique et Sociétés* 16/1: 39–59.

Betsill, Michele and Elisabeth Corell (eds.). 2008. *NGO Diplomacy: The Influence of Nongovernmental Organizations in International Environmental Negotiations.* Cambridge: MIT Press.

Bhabha, Homi K. 1984. "Of Mimicry and Man: The Ambivalence of Colonial Discourse." *October*, 28: 125–133.

Bizoux, Angélique. 2006. *Catalogne: l'émergence d'une politique extérieure.* Strasbourg: L'Harmattan.

Bjola, Corneliu. 2013. "Understanding Enmity and Friendship in World Politics: the Case for a Diplomatic Approach. " *The Hague Journal of Diplomacy* 8: 1–20.

Black, Jeremy. 2010. *A History of Diplomacy.* London: Reaktion Books.

Brennan, T. Corey. 2009. "Embassies gone wrong: Roman diplomacy in the Constantinian Excerpta De Legationibus." In *Diplomats and Diplomacy in the Roman World*, edited by Claude Eilers, 171–192. Leiden: Brill.

Brubaker, Rogers. 2004. *Ethnicity Without Groups.* Cambridge: Harvard University Press.

Bursens, Peter and Jana Deforche. 2010. "Going beyond paradiplomacy? Adding historical institutionalism to account for regional foreign policy competences." *The Hague Journal of Diplomacy* 5 (1–2): 151–171.

Butler, Rohan. 1961. "Paradiplomacy." In *Studies in Diplomatic History and Historiography in Honor of G.P. Gooch*, edited by Arshag O. Sarkissian, 12–25. London: Longman.

Cantir, Cristian. 2015. "Russian-Backed Paradiplomacy in the 'Near Abroad': Gagauzia, Moldova and the Rift over European Integration." *The Hague Journal of Diplomacy* 10: 261–284.

Cardinal, Mario. 2005. *Breaking Point: Quebec, Canada, The 1995 Referendum*. Montreal: Bayard Canada Books.

Carod-Rovira, Josep. 2009. *El papel de Catalunya en l'Europa del segle XXI*. Barcelona: C.l.d.i. conferències, Generalitat de Catalunya.

———. 2010. "Introduction." In *Catalonia Foreign Affairs Strategy*, edited by the Generalitat de Catalunya, 11. Barcelona: Generalitat de Catalunya.

Constantinou, Costas. 2009. "On homo-diplomacy." *Space and Culture* 9: 351–364.

Constantinou, Costas and James Der Derian. 2010. "Sustaining Global Hope: Sovereignty, Power and the Transformation of Diplomacy." In *Sustainable Diplomacies*, edited by Costas Constantinou and James Der Derian, 1–22. Basingstoke: Palgrave Macmillan.

Constantinou, Costas. 2010. "Diplomacy, Spirituality, Alterity." In *Sustainable Diplomacies*, edited by Costas Constantinou and James der Derian, 67–88. Basingstoke: Palgrave Macmillan.

Cornago, Noé. 2010a. "On the Normalization of Sub-state Diplomacy." *The Hague Journal of Diplomacy*, 5,1–2: 11–36.

———. 2010b. "Perforated Sovereignties, Agonistic Pluralism and the Durability of (Para)Diplomacy." In *Sustainable Diplomacies*, edited by Costas Constantinou and James Der Derian, 89–108. Basingstoke: Palgrave Macmillan.

———. 2010c. *Exploring the global dimensions of paradiplomacy: Functional and normative dynamics in the global spreading of subnational involvement in the international affairs*. Ottawa: Forum des federations.

———. 2013. "(Para)Diplomatic Cultures: Old and New". Paper presented at the International Workshop "Alternative Cultures of Diplomacy, UNPO/The Hague, November, 2013.

Criekemans, David, Manuel Duran and Jan Melissen. 2009. *Towards a 'third wave' in sub-state diplomacy?* Antwerp: Policy Research Center on Foreign Policy.

Criekemans, David and Manuel Duran. 2010. "Small state diplomacy compared to sub-state diplomacy: more of the same or different?" In *Small states in Europe: challenges and opportunities*, edited by Robert Steinmetz et al., 31–46. Farnham: Ashgate.

Criekemans, David. 2010a. "Regional sub-state diplomacy from a comparative perspective: Quebec, Scotland, Bavaria, Catalonia, Wallonia and Flanders." In *Regional sub-state diplomacy today*, edited by David Criekemans, 37–64. Leiden: Martinus Nijhoff.

———. 2010b. *Foreign Policy and Diplomacy of the Belgian Regions: Flanders and Wallonia*. The Hague: Clingendael Discussion Papers in Diplomacy.

Delmartino, Frank. 2011. "The international policy of Flanders." In *Autonomie régionale et relations internationals*, edited by Carlos E. Pacheco Amaral, 45–74. Paris: L'Harmattan.

Denza, Eileen. 2004. *Diplomatic law: Commentary on the Vienna Convention on Diplomatic Relations*. Oxford: Oxford University Press.

Duchacek, Ivo. 1986. *The territorial dimension of politics within, among and across nations*. Boulder: Westview Press.

Duchacek, Ivo D. 1990. "Perforated Sovereignties: Towards a Typology of New Actors in International Relations." In *Federalism and International Relations. The Role of Subnational Units*, edited by Hans Michelmann and Panayotis Soldatos, 1–34. Oxford: Clarendon Press.

Duran, Manuel, David Criekemans and Jan Melissen. 2008. *Een vergelijkend onderzoek naar en bestedingsanalyse van het buitenlands beleid en de diplomatieke representatie van regio's met wetgevende bevoegdheid en kleine staten.* Antwerpen: Vlaams Steunpunt Buitenlands Beleid.

Duran, Manuel. 2013. "An archaeology of Mediterranean diplomacy: the evidence of paradiplomacy." *International journal of Euro-Mediterranean Studies* 5: 147–158.

———. 2015. *Mediterranean Paradiplomacies. Dynamics of Diplomatic Reterritorialization.* Boston: Brill.

Elazar, Daniel. 1987. *Exploring Federalism*. Tuscaloosa: University of Alabama Press.

Fleming, Chris. 2004. *René Girard: Violence and Mimesis*. Cambridge: Polity.

Foucault, Michel. 1981. "The Order of Discourse." In *Untying the Text: A Post-Structuralist Reader*, edited by Robert Young, 48–78. Boston, London, Henley: Routledge & Kegan Paul.

Fresa, Matilde. 2006. "Le politiche della Regione Emilia-Romagna con il popolo saharawi: Una 'borderlinking line' tra cooperazione decentrata e paradiplomacy." *Afriche e orienti: rivista Di studia i confini tra Africa, Mediterraneo e Medio Oriente*, 3–4.

Girard, René. 1977. *Violence and the Sacred.* Baltimore: The Johns Hopkins University Press.

———. 1996. *Quand les choses commenceront. Entretiens avec Michel Treguer*. Paris: Arléa.

Gray, David. 2009. *Doing Research in the Real World.* London: Sage.

Grydehœj, Adam. 2014. "Goals, capabilities, and instruments of paradiplomacy by subnational jurisdictions." In *Paradiplomacy*, edited by Adam Grydehœj et al., 10–21. Brussels: Centre Maurits Coppieters.

Guerrero i Tarragó, Marc. 2007. *La identitat en l'actuació exterior subestatal: Actuacions governementals de Catalunya i de l'estat de Washington.* Ph.D for the Departement de sociologia i analisi de les organitzacions Barcelona. Barcelona: University of Barcelona.

Hansen, Thomas Blom and Finn Stepputat. 2001. *States of Imagination: Ethnographic Explorations of the Postcolonial State*. Durham: Duke University Press.

Hocking, Brian. 1993. *Localizing Foreign Policy. Non-Central Governments and Multilayered Diplomacy*. New York: St. Martin's Press.

———. 1995. "Beyond 'newness' and 'decline': the development of catalytic diplomacy." *Diplomatic Studies Programme Discussion Paper* (DSPDP) 10, Diplomatic Studies Programme, Leicester University.

———. 1999. "Patrolling the 'Frontier': Globalization, Localization and the 'Actorness' of Non-Central Governments." In *Paradiplomacy In Action: The Foreign Relations of Subnational Governments*, edited by Fransisco Aldecoa and Michael Keating, 17–39. London: Frank Cass.

Hocking, Brian et al. 2013. *Futures for diplomacy. Integrative Diplomacy in the 21st Century*. The Hague: Netherlands Institute of International Relations 'Clingendael'.

Izzo, Marina. 2006. *Questioni e prospettive della cooperazione decentrata dall' Andalusia alla Toscana. Un'indagine sulla governance multilivello*, CeSPI Working Papers 27/2006.

Jacobson, Jon. 1994. *When the Soviet Union entered world politics*. Berkeley: University of California Press.

Keating, Michael. 1999. "Regions and International Affairs: Motives, Opportunities and Strategies." *Regional and Federal Studies* 9/1: 1–16.

———. 2001. *Plurinational Democracy: Stateless Nations in a Post-Sovereign Era*. Oxford: Oxford University Press.

Kenealy, Daniel. 2012. "Commercial Interests and Calculated Compassion: The Diplomacy and Paradiplomacy of Releasing the Lockerbie Bomber." *Diplomacy and Statecraft* 23: 555–575.

Khanna, Parag. 2011. *How to Run The World: Charting a Course to the Next Renaissance*. New York: Random House.

Kocho-Williams, Alastair. 2012. *Russian and Soviet Diplomacy, 1900–39*. Basingstoke: Palgrave MacMillan.

Kuznetsov, Alexander. 2015. *Theory and Practice of Paradiplomacy: Subnational Governments in International Affairs*. Milton Park: Routledge.

Lachapelle, Guy and Stéphane Paquin. 2013. "Quebec' international strategies: mastering globalization and new possibilities of governance." Paper presented at the Conference Québec and Canada in the New Century: New Dynamics, New Opportunities Queen's University School of Policy Studies, 31 October–1 November 2003.

Lancaster, Carol. 2007. *Foreign Aid: Diplomacy, Development, Domestic Politics*. Chicago: University of Chicago Press.

Lecours, André. 2002. "Paradiplomacy: Reflections on the Foreign Policy and International Relations of Regions." *International Negotiation* 7/1: 91–114.

———. 2008. "Political Issues of Paradiplomacy: Lessons from the Developed World." In *Discussion Papers on Diplomacy*, edited by Virginie Duthoit and Ellen Huijgh. The Hague: Netherlands Institute of International Relations 'Clingendael'.

Lohmar Sainz de Vicuña, Ramón. 2015. "Catalan Paradiplomacy, Secessionism and State Sovereignty. The Effects of the 2006 Statute of Autonomy and the Artur Mas Government on Catalan Paradiplomacy." MA thesis, University of Leiden.

Marks, Gary, Liesbet Hooghe and Arjan H Schakel. 2008. "Measuring regional authority." *Regional and Federal Studies* 18 (2–3): 111–121.

McConnell, Fiona, Terri Moreau, and Jason Dittmer. 2012. "Mimicking state diplomacy: The legitimizing strategies of unofficial diplomacies." *Geoforum*, 43/4: 804–814.

Melissen, Jan. 1999. *Innovation in diplomatic practice*. Basingstoke New York: Palgrave.

Mintz, Alex and Karl DeRouen. 2010. Understanding foreign policy decision making. Cambridge: Cambridge University Press.

Mouffe, Chantal. 2013. *Agonistics. Thinking the World Politically*. London: Verso.

Nicolson, Harold. 1962. *The Evolution of Diplomacy*. Springfield: Collier Books.

Nietzsche, Friedrich. 2013. *On the Genealogy of Morals*, translated by Michael A. Scarpitti and edited by Robert C. Holub. New York: Penguin Classics.

Paquin, Stéphane. 2003. *Paradiplomatie identitaire en Catalogne*. Québec: Les Presses de l' Université Laval.

———. 2004. *Paradiplomatie et relations internationales: Théorie des strategies internationales des regions face à la mondialisation*. Brussel: P.I.E.-Peter Lang.

Paquin Stéphane and Guy Lachapelle. 2005. "Why do sub-states and regions practice international relations?" In *Mastering Globalization. New substates' governance and strategies*, edited by Guy Lachapelle and Stephane Paquin, 77–89. London and New York: Routledge.

Pauwels, Jacques R. 2014. *De Groote Klassenoorlog 1914–1918*. Berchem: EPO Uitgeverij.

Petric, Ernest. 2013. Foreign Policy: from conception to diplomatic practice. Leiden and Boston: Martinus Nijhoff.

Philippart, Eric. 1998. "Gouvernance à niveaux multiples et relations extérieures: le développement de la 'paradiplomatie' au sein de l'Union européenne et la nouvelle donne belge." *Revue Études internationales* XXIX/3: 631–646.

Pipes, Richard. 1991. *The Russian Revolution*. New York: Vintage Books.

Pujol, Jordi. 2011. "Interview with Jordi Pujol." In *What Catalans Want?*, edited by Toni Strubell, 54–59. Ashfield: Catalonia Press.

Rana, Kishan S. 2011. 21st Century Diplomacy. A practitioner's guide. London and New York: Bloomsbury.

Regione, Emilia-Romagna. 2010. Progetti di cooperazione internazionale, pace e diritti umani. Bologna: Servizio Politiche Europee e Relazioni Internazionali.

Riordan, Shaun. 2002. *The New Diplomacy*. Cambridge: Polity Press.

Rutan, Gerard. 1971. "Provincial Participation in Canadian Foreign Relations." *Journal of Interamerican Studies and World Affairs* 13(2): 230–245.

Satow, Ernest Mason. 1932. *A guide to diplomatic practice*. London: Longmans.

Schacter, Noel, Jim Beebe and Luigi Zanasi. 2004. *Globalization and the North: Impacts of Trade Treaties on Canada's Northern Governments*. Ottawa: Canadian Centre for Policy Alternatives.

Sharp, Paul. 2009. *Diplomatic Theory of International Relations*. Cambridge: Cambridge University Press.

Soldatos, Panayotis. 1990. "An Explanatory Framework for the Study of Federated States as Foreign-policy Actors." In *Federalism and International Relations. The Role of Subnational Units*, edited by Hans Michelmann and Panayotis Soldatos, 34–53. Oxford: Clarendon Press.

Stavridis, Stelios. 2002. "The Parliamentary Forum of the Euro-Mediterranean Partnership: An Assessment." *Mediterranean Politics* 7(2): 30–53.

———. 2007. "Parliamentary Diplomacy: Any Lessons for Regional Parliaments?" In *Las relaciones internacionales de las regiones: actores sub-nacionales, para-diplomacia y gobernanza multinivel / The International Relations of the Regions: Subnational Actors, Paradiplomacy and Multilevel Governance*, edited by M. Kölling, S. Stavridis and N. Fernandez Sola, 55–81. Zaragoza: Universidad de Zaragoza.

Stocchiero, Andrea. 2007. *I nodi dell'evoluzione della cooperazione decentrata italiana*, CeSPI Working Papers 37/2007.

Van Alstein, Maarten. 2011. *The Great War Remembered: Commemoration and Peace in Flanders Fields*. Brussels: Flemish Peace Institute.

Velaers, Jan. 2006. "'In foro interno, in foro externo': De internationale bevoegdheden van gemeenschappen en gewesten." In *Internationale Betrekkingen*, edited by Frank Judo and Godfried Geudens, 3–86. Ghent: Larcier.

Verbruggen, Didier. 2015. *Vredesopbouw en conflictpreventie in het Vlaamse buitenland-beleid: een blauwdruk voor de inzet van expertise*. Brussels: Vlaams Vredesinstituut.

Waeterloos, Evert. 2008. *Vlaamse ontwikkelingssamenwerking en de zoektocht naar doeltreffende hulp*. Antwerp: Vlaams Steunpunt Buitenlands Beleid.

Wernick, Andrew. 1999. *Bataille's Columbine: The Sacred Space Of Hate*, online article, Centre for the Study of Theory, published 11/3/1999.

Wheeler-Bennett, John W. 1938. "The Meaning of Brest-Litovsk Today." *Foreign Affairs*, October 1938: 137–152.

Zanon, Bruno. 2011. "Infrastructure Network Development, Re-territorialization Processes and Multilevel Territorial Governance: A Case Study in Northern Italy." *Planning Practice and Research* 26(3): 325–347.

Further Reading

Criekemans, David, ed. (2010). *Regional sub- state diplomacy today*. Leiden: Martinus Nijhoff. A very insightful reader of paradiplomacy, with a variety of perspectives and vantage points, ranging from historical institutionalism and IR-theory, to a practitioner's standpoint and a comparative study of paradiplomatic practices. David Criekemans offers an excellent introduction to the literature and practice of paradiplomacy.

Kuznetsov, Alexander. (2015). *Theory and Practice of Paradiplomacy: Subnational Governments in International Affairs*. Milton Park: Routledge. The author presents a comprehensive and complete theoretical framework of paradiplomacy. The book is well embedded in IR- theory and Federalism Studies.

Cornago, Noé. (2013). *Plural Diplomacies: Normative Predicaments and Functional Imperatives*. Leiden/Boston: Brill. Paradiplomacy is presented by Noé Cornago as one of the many faces/instances of the manifold of diplomacies that characterize our current international landscape. The author also offers an unconventional diachronic insight in the historical genesis of paradiplomacy and other sites of diplomatic encounters.

Michelmann, Hans, ed. (2009). *Foreign Relations in Federal Countries*. Montreal and Kingston: McGill-Queen's University Press and Forum of Federations. A very insightful overview and comparison of a number of paradiplomacies around the world.

Lecours, Andre. (2002). "Paradiplomacy: Reflections on the Foreign Policy and International Relations of Regions". *International Negotiation* 7(1): 91–114. André Lecours analyses paradiplomacy from the vantage point of political opportunity structures, at three governance levels: the national, the European and the international/global. In doing so, he presents an explanatory framework for the study of paradiplomacy.

Setzer, Joana. (2014). "How Subnational Governments are Rescaling Environmental Governance: The Case of the Brazilian State of Sao Paolo." *Journal of Environmental Policy and Planning* April: 1–17. The impact of sub-state diplomacy on environmental policies and vice versa. A still rather unknown aspect of paradiplomacy, but one with an increasing relevance.

Fry, Earl. H. (2013). "Relating Cities to their International Context." *Handbook of Research Methods and Applications in Urban Economies*, eds. Peter Karl Kresl and Jaime Sobrino, 175–208. Edward Elgar. Cities are increasingly playing a major role in the current diplomatic setting. Earl Fry offers an insightful analysis of their international activities.

Dickson, Francesca. (2014). "The Internationalization of Regions: Paradiplomacy or Multi-Level Governance?" *Geography Compass* 8(10): 689–700. Especially in a European context, paradiplomacy has become part and parcel of a complex and rich multi-level political and diplomatic governance model. Dickson takes stock of the basic concepts, differences and similarities between paradiplomacy and multi-level governance.

Royles, Elin. (2010). "Small, Smart, Successful: A Nation Influencing the Twenty-First-Century World? The Emerging Welsh Paradiplomacy." *Contemporary Wales* 23(1): 142–170. The British devolved territories have become a laboratory for modern paradiplomacy. Most attention goes to Scotland, but also Wales and Northern Ireland have developed their own system of paradiplomacy. Elin Royles paints a picture of a small but smart sub-state international actor.

Acuto, Michele. (2013). *Global Cities, Governance, and Diplomacy: The Urban Link.* Oxford: Routledge. The most complete overview of the way in which cities are carving out a place for their own in the global mega-diplomatic world, with a special emphasis on the importance of networks and the variety of city governance models.

Van den Brande, L. (2010). "Sub-State Diplomacy Today: A Practitioner's View." *The Hague Journal of Diplomacy* 5(1): 191–210. This account of the practice of paradiplomacy by a practitioner is a rarity; well-written and very insightful testimony by former Flemish Prime Minister Luc Van den Brande, also the architect of Flemish paradiplomacy during the 1990s.

Tatham, Michael. (2014). "Same Game but More Players? Sub-national Lobbying in an Enlarged Union." *Regional and Federal Studies* 24(3): 341–361. Sub-state entities as actors of international and European lobbying. The author presents the practice of paradiplomacy as a form of interest group lobbying.

www.ingramcontent.com/pod-product-compliance
Lightning Source LLC
Chambersburg PA
CBHW031334230926
51848CB00001B/226
* 9 7 8 9 0 0 4 3 2 5 9 2 0 *